Evaluating Eden Series No. 2 (IIED)
Occasional Publication No. 46 (CCI Press)

NORTHERN EDEN

Community-based wildlife management in Canada

Leslie Treseder
Jamie Honda-McNeil
Mina Berkes
Fikret Berkes
Joe Dragon
Claudia Notzke
Tanja Schramm
Robert J. Hudson

Canadian Circumpolar Institute (CCI) Press
Occasional Publication No. 46
ISBN 1-896445-14-4
ISSN 0068-0303; 46
North American rights
© 1999

Canadian Cataloguing in Publication Data

Main entry under title:
   Northern Eden

   (Occasional publication / Canadian Circumpolar Institute,
   ISSN 0068-0303 ; no. 46)
   Includes bibliographical references and index.
   ISBN 1-896445-14-4

   1. Wildlife management—Canada. 2. Wildlife management
   —Canada—Citizen participation. 3. Native peoples—Canada.*
   I. Treseder, Leslie. II. Canadian Circumpolar Institute.
   III. Series: Occasional publication
   (Canadian Circumpolar Institute) ; no. 46.

   SK471.N6N67 1999   333.95'4'0971   C99-911170-1

© 1999 Canadian Circumpolar Institute (CCI) Press
North American rights.

ISBN 1-896445-14-4
Occasional Publication No. 46

Canadian Circumpolar Institute Press
This Canadian printing of this publication was made possible with
funding from the Environment and Renewable Resources Directorate,
Northern Affairs Program, Department of Indian Affairs and Northern
Development; and the Office of the Federal Negotiator for Nunavik,
Department of Indian Affairs and Northern Development, Canada.

Published in the UK by the International Institute for Environment
and Development (IIED), 3 Ensleigh Road, London WC1H 0DD, UK.
ISBN 1561-8382
IIED — Evaluating Eden Series, No. 2

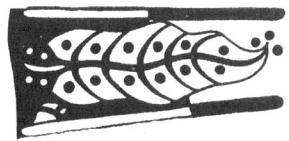 # Acknowledgements

This report was made possible by a grant from IIED in London, England, along with office, administrative, and graduate student assistance from the University of Alberta in Edmonton, Canada. The printing of this Canadian edition was made possible with funding from the Environment and Renewable Resources Directorate, Northern Affairs Program, Department of Indian Affairs and Northern Development; and the Office of the Federal Negotiator for Nunavik, Department of Indian Affairs and Northern Development, Canada.

This Canadian contribution to the "Evaluating Eden" project was a team effort, and a list of contributors is included at the back of this report. We have divided our team into "authors," "advisors," and "other contributors," although many of us served more than one role. The principal authors of this report were Leslie Treseder, Jamie Honda-McNeil, Mina Berkes, Fikret Berkes, Joe Dragon, Claudia Notzke, Tanja Schramm, and Robert J. Hudson. Advisors who offered support and suggestions were Milton Freeman, Naomi Krogman, and Dilys Roe.

Other contributors provided invaluable assistance during preparation of this report:

- Norm Mair of the NWT Centre for Remote Sensing, Yellowknife, Northwest Territories, prepared the maps of Canada and of the comprehensive claim settlement areas.

- External reviewers Dr. Anne Gunn (Ungulate Biologist, NWT Department of Resources, Wildlife and Economic Development, Yellowknife, Northwest Territories), and Dr. Lee Foote (Sessional Lecturer, Department of Renewable Resources, University of Alberta, Edmonton, Alberta) provided constructive criticism of the first draft.

- Several sources of unpublished data were used in this report. We thank authors Joe Dragon and Claudia Notzke, along with other contributors, for enabling use of this information.

- Fikret Berkes and Jamie Honda-McNeil provided advice and comments for Chapter 6.

- Administrative and project management assistance were provided by Robert Hudson in Edmonton and Dilys Roe in London.

- An annotated bibliography on *Involvement of Aboriginal People in Environmental and Renewable Resource Management in Canada* was provided to IIED to accompany this report. The bibliography was made available by The Policy and Public Involvement Branch, Saskatchewan Environment and Resource Management, Saskatoon, Saskatchewan.

The opinions expressed herein are those of the authors and are not necessarily shared by the Canadian Circumpolar Institute at the University of Alberta or the International Institute for Environment and Development. Considerable revisions were made to this report following review of the first draft and I take full responsibility for any errors or omissions in the final report.

Leslie Treseder
Project Coordinator
Department of Renewable Resources
University of Alberta, Edmonton

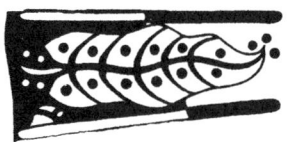

Contents

Abbreviations vi

Introduction 1

Chapter 1:
The evolution and status of wildlife co-management in Canada
by Leslie Treseder and Jamie Honda-McNeil 5

Chapter 2:
Subsistence hunting of wildlife in the Canadian north
by Mina Berkes and Fikret Berkes 21

Chapter 3:
Commercial harvesting of wild ungulates in northern Canada
by Joe Dragon 33

Chapter 4:
Aboriginal community involvement in wildlife tourism: The Canadian experience
by Claudia Notzke 45

Chapter 5:
The status of game ranching among Canada's Aboriginal people
by Tanja Schramm and Robert J. Hudson 63

Chapter 6:
Reflections on Canadian experience in community-based wildlife management
by Leslie Treseder 75

References 79
About the Authors 89
Index 91

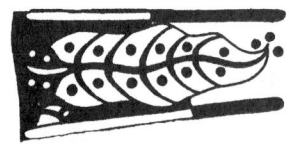

Abbreviations

BQCMB	Beverly-Qamanirjuaq Caribou Management Board
CFIA	Canadian Food Inspection Agency
CITES	Convention on International Trade in Endangered Species
COSEWIC	Committee on the Status of Endangered Wildlife in Canada
DIAND	Department of Indian Affairs & Northern Development
FJMC	Fisheries Joint Management Committee
GAE	Guided Arctic Expeditions
GHL	General Hunting License
GNWT	Government of the Northwest Territories
HTA	Hunters' and Trappers' Association
HTC	Hunters' and Trappers' Committee
ICC	Indian Claims Commission
ICS	Inuvialuit Communications Society
IFA	Inuvialuit Final Agreement
IGC	Inuvialuit Game Council
IIED	International Institute for Environment and Development
ISR	Inuvialuit Settlement Region
ITBC	Inter Tribal Bison Cooperative
JBNQA	James Bay and Northern Quebec Agreement
LIA	Labrador Inuit Association
LIDC	Labrador Inuit Development Corporation
MFNEBC	Manitoba First Nations Elk and Bison Council
NRC	National Research Council (Canada)
NWT	Northwest Territories
ODA	Overseas Development Administration
RCAP	Royal Commission on Aboriginal Peoples
RWED	Resources, Wildlife and Economic Development (GNWT)
SCONE	Special Committee on the Northern Economy
TAH	Total Allowable Harvest
TEK	Traditional Ecological Knowledge

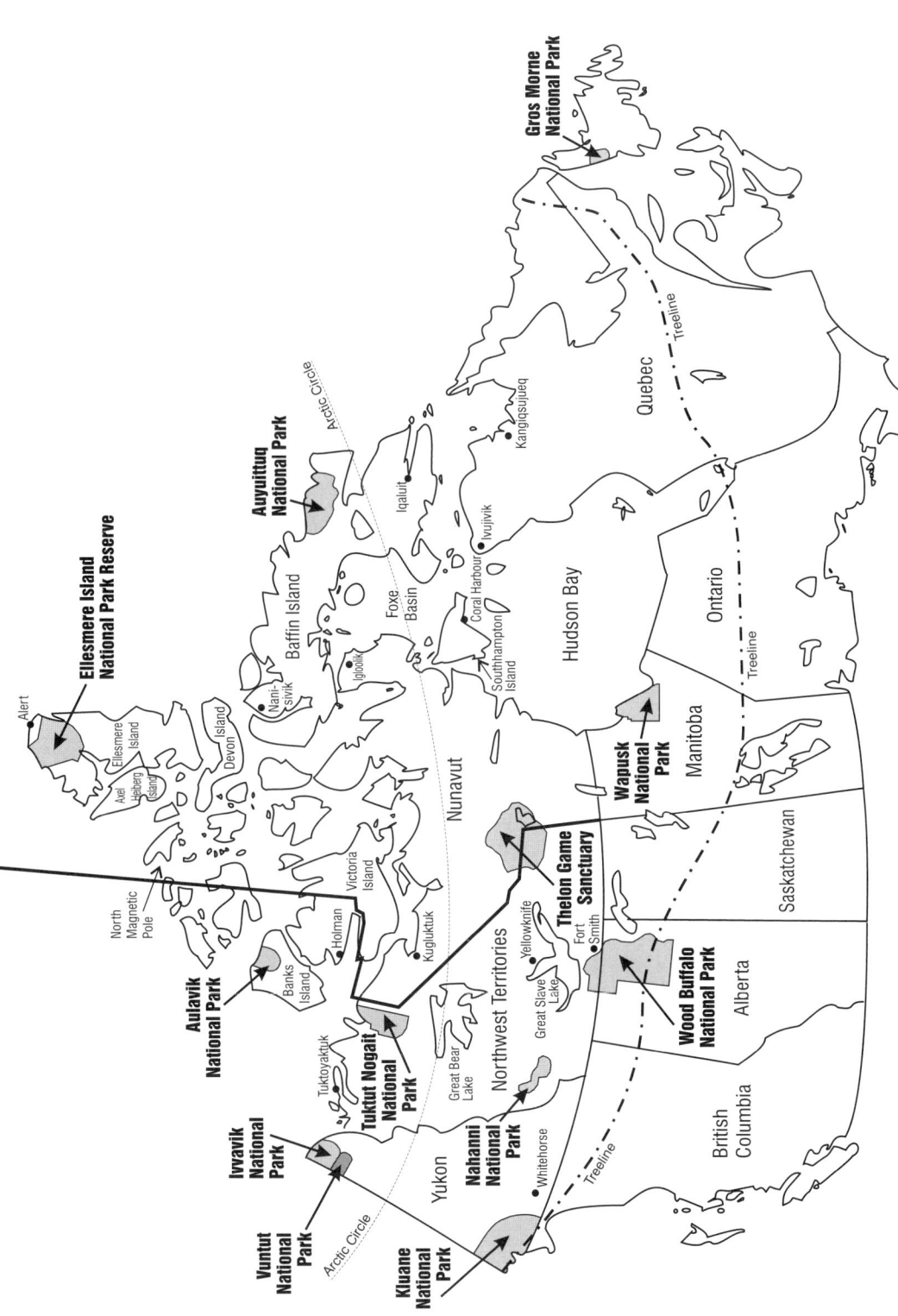

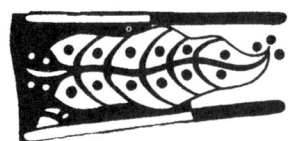

Introduction

Canada is the world's second-largest country, covering an area of 9,970,610 square kilometres. In 1996, the total population of Canada was 28,846,761.[1] Most of this population is concentrated close to Canada's southern border (with the United States), in urban/industrialized, and agricultural areas. To the north of these areas lie the vast, sparsely-populated boreal forest and arctic (tundra) regions. These regions of low biological productivity continue to support large populations of free-roaming wildlife. These wildlife resources have sustained northern Aboriginal societies for thousands of years and continue to play an important role in the economic, social, and cultural life of Canada's northern communities.

Most of Canada's northern communities are small (<1,000), largely Aboriginal, and dependent to varying degrees on wildlife for food. These communities are widely scattered, geographically remote from non-Aboriginal population centres, and located in relatively pristine environments. Their populations are young and growing at a rapid rate compared to the rest of the population. By national standards, Canada's northern communities possess very modest physical infrastructures and many are inaccessible by road. These communities are characterized by high costs of living and mixed economies based on a mix of subsistence activities, wage employment, private enterprise, and transfer payments.

Management of wildlife in Canada is derived from the Roman principle of *res nullius*. Wildlife has no owner until captured or killed, and is managed by the Crown (state) on behalf of all citizens. Private land owners may control access for hunting wildlife, but in most cases do not "own" the wildlife on their land. Management of wildlife and habitat is largely a provincial responsibility, with the Federal Government having a mandate for management of migratory and endangered species. In Canada's northern territories, the territorial governments are responsible for management of wildlife, but the Federal Government owns much of the land, and is therefore responsible for habitat management.

---

1. Data from the 1996 Census of Canada are available via the internet from Statistics Canada (www.statcan.ca).

Aboriginal people own large tracts of land in Canada's northern territories, which they acquired under comprehensive (land) claim settlements. Comprehensive claim settlements represent modern attempts to deal with long-standing Aboriginal claims related to land and resources. The comprehensive claims process has given Canada's northern Aboriginal people legislated access to both wildlife resources and shared decision-making. These access rights apply not only to Aboriginal lands, but also to other areas (Crown lands) covered by comprehensive claim settlements. Canada's northern Aboriginal people have thus achieved security of tenure with respect to wildlife, an important theme of other regional reviews in the "Evaluating Eden" project (see Kothari *et al.* 1997). Through the comprehensive claims process, Canada's northern Aboriginal people have reformed the conventional government approach to wildlife management. They have secured access to both resources and decision-making, and have protected land for use rather than from use (see Pimbert and Pretty 1997).

Some of Canada's Aboriginal people have special rights to wildlife, derived from historical agreements. Canadian Indian and Inuit people[2] generally have hunting rights that are subject to limitation only by the Federal Government, and then only in the interests of conservation or public safety. Other Canadian Aboriginal people, the non-status Indians and Métis[3], have no special rights to wildlife at this time. In this paper, Aboriginal usually means Indian and Inuit, although the Métis may be included in some cases. The terms Aboriginal, indigenous, and Native are used interchangeably.

The rights of Canada's Aboriginal people to wildlife do not imply ownership, and the Crown always retains an interest in wildlife management. There are no cases where wildlife management has been completely delegated to communities, as ministers of government

---

2. North American Indians are descendants of the Indian Nations inhabiting North America before European contact. Historically, Indian Nations inhabited all parts of Canada south of the treeline (the transition between boreal forest and tundra). The Inuit lived mostly in tundra areas north of the treeline.

3. "Non-status" Indians are individuals who, for various reasons, have lost their Treaty status, meaning they are no longer recognized under the terms of treaties made between governments and Indian Nations. Métis people have part-Indian ancestry. The Métis were recognized in some early constitutional documents, but have a land base only in the Province of Alberta (see Notzke 1994).

Introduction

always retain their legislative authority. Community-based wildlife management in Canada is therefore carried out in this context. In Canada's northern territories, the dominant system for wildlife management is co-management through the comprehensive claims process. Co-management through comprehensive claims involves *"sharing of power and responsibilities between government and local resource users"* (Berkes et al. 1991). Co-management also exists outside of the comprehensive claims process, but its definition and application vary widely across the country. This latter type of wildlife co-management does not have the same legislative basis (as comprehensive claims) and may be known by a variety of terms including cooperative management, collaborative management, joint management, participatory management, and multi-stakeholder management (Berkes 1997).

This report consists of a series of essays on various aspects of community-based wildlife management in Canada, with a focus on co-management of terrestrial mammals in Canada's northern territories. Chapter 1 provides some historical background on Aboriginal wildlife rights and the comprehensive claims process, and also discusses the current status of wildlife co-management in Canada. Chapters 2 through 5 examine four specific wildlife-based activities being undertaken by northern Canadian communities:

- **Subsistence hunting** (Chapter 2)—hunting for food and maintenance of social and cultural relationships;
- **Commercial hunting** (Chapter 3)—hunting for sale of meat to local and/or export markets;
- **Wildlife tourism** (Chapter 4)—selling of wildlife-related experiences to visitors;
- **Game ranching** (Chapter 5)—management of ungulates for breeding stock, trophy hunting and/or production of meat and other products.

Chapter 6 attempts to draw some conclusions related to the "Evaluating Eden" project.

There are many overlaps between the different wildlife-based activities described in Chapters 2 through 5, and we have divided them based more on our expertise than on clear (or agreed-upon) distinctions between them. These essays were not edited for consistency of views as we hope to reflect not only the diversity of Canadian experience but also the variety of opinions on wildlife co-management and related issues. We hope that this diversity can make a contribution to the "Evaluating Eden" project and offer some experience to other communities involved in wildlife management projects or seeking a voice in wildlife management decision-making.

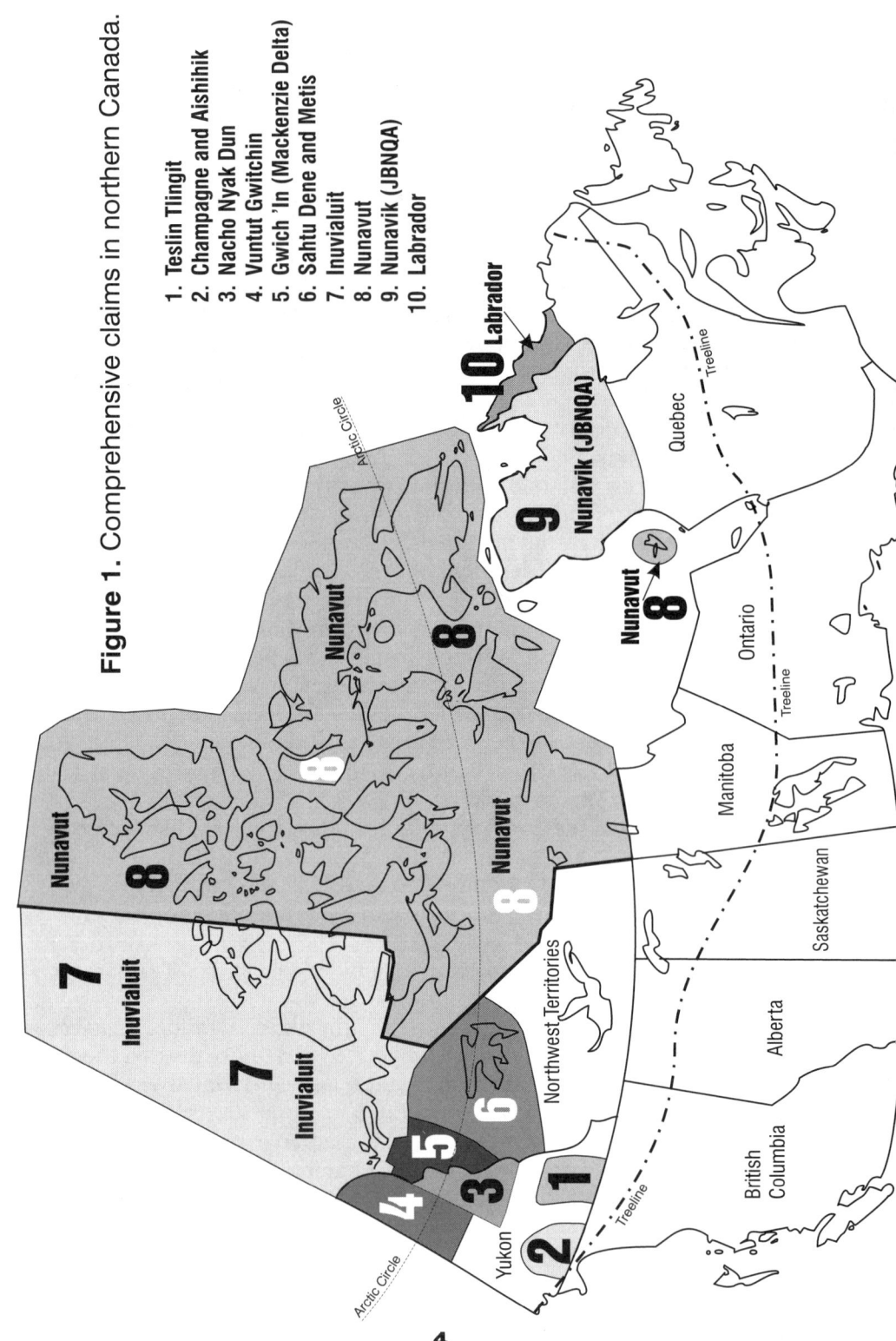

Figure 1. Comprehensive claims in northern Canada.

1. Teslin Tlingit
2. Champagne and Aishihik
3. Nacho Nyak Dun
4. Vuntut Gwitchin
5. Gwich 'In (Mackenzie Delta)
6. Sahtu Dene and Metis
7. Inuvialuit
8. Nunavut
9. Nunavik (JBNQA)
10. Labrador

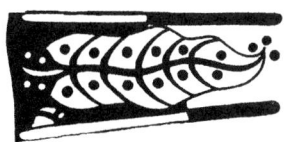

CHAPTER 1:

The evolution and status of wildlife co-management in Canada

Leslie Treseder and Jamie Honda-McNeil

The present system of wildlife co-management in Canada developed as a result of many interrelated factors. These factors include continued community dependence on wildlife, a favourable legal regime, and public and administrative support for involving resource users in wildlife management decision-making. The rights of local resource users to wildlife in Canada are intimately related to the broader topic of Aboriginal rights. Chapter 1 therefore presents a brief history of Aboriginal rights Canada, providing some legal and political context for development of the present co-management system. The history presented in this paper is neither a legal interpretation nor a complete representation of existing information. Rather, it highlights some important historical events which have affected the present status of Canadian Aboriginal people with respect of wildlife resources. Chapter 1 also provides a brief overview of the current status of wildlife co-management in Canada, including key issues, current trends, and future directions.

1.1 Royal policy and early treaties

The history of Canada is not one of wars and conquest, but rather of European "discovery" and settlement of a land already occupied by Indian and Inuit peoples. European colonists established their presence

in what is now Canada by making treaties with the various Indian nations occupying the land.[4] Treaties served many purposes, including:
- resolution of land ownership, enabling European governments to claim or grant lands;
- resolution of issues related to sharing of land and resources;
- cementing of commercial and military enterprises between European governments and Aboriginal people (Hamilton 1995).

Treaty-making was no doubt an important part of military strategy during the early days of Canadian settlement, and was essential to the security of both Aboriginal people and early colonizers.

Fig. 2. *Treaty 8 commemorative medal. These medals were given to Indian leaders who signed Treaty 8 in 1899. Photo by D. Hyduk, Provincial Archives of Alberta courtesy of the Ethnology Collection H86.49.1, Provincial Museum of Alberta.*

By 1763, the British Crown had assumed control of the territory that was to become Canada, and issued a policy to govern relations between Aboriginal peoples, the colonists, and the Crown (Elias 1989). The *Royal Proclamation of 1763*, issued by King George III, reserved lands to the Indians as their hunting grounds. They were not to be disturbed in their use or enjoyment of their lands. A process of acquiring land for settlement, including public meetings and Aboriginal consent, was to be followed by all Agents of the Crown (Royal Proclamation October 7, 1763; see Hamilton 1995).

---

4. One of the first treaties in North America was made in 1699 between the Six Nations Iroquois and the Dutch Crown. Known as the "Two Row Wampum," this Treaty signified that each signatory would never interfere in the affairs of the other (Hamilton 1995). Treaties were made between various European governments and Indian Nations throughout North America. Treaties were never made between European governments and Indian nations in some regions of Canada, or between European governments and the Inuit.

The evolution and status of wildlife co-management in Canada

The Royal Proclamation of 1763 is a most significant document in the history of Aboriginal rights in Canada (ICC 1975). This document has been called an early comprehensive claims policy (Daniel 1980) and a Charter of Indian Rights (Alberta Native Affairs 1986). It is the foundation of treaties made with Aboriginal people both before and after Canadian Confederation[5] (ICC 1975, Hamilton 1995). Each of the early treaties was worded somewhat differently. Most contained assurances of the rights of Aboriginal people to live as they did before and to continue their usual vocations (Hamilton 1995, Makowecki 1993). Some included reservation of lands for Indian use in exchange for surrender or extinguishment of Aboriginal title.

Modern interpretations of King George III's intentions include keeping the Indians as allies during times of war and trading partners during times of peace (Hamilton 1995), and avoiding or minimizing hostilities over encroachments on Indian lands (Alberta Native Affairs 1986, Daniel 1980). Certainly the treaty-making process was essential to maintaining peace with the Indians during the often-turbulent settlement of western Canada. By the mid-1800s, however, the spirit and intent of the Royal Proclamation were beginning to fade in face of the practical needs of colonial growth. In spite of support for Indian rights within the North American justice system, Indians were routinely dispossessed of their lands in order to remove obstacles to an expanding frontier[6] (Elias 1989). The expanding frontier also encroached on Indians' ability to continue their usual vocations and marked the

---

5. 'Confederation' refers to the union of two different regions to form what is now Canada. In 1867, the union of Canada—parts of present-day Quebec and Ontario, New Brunswick and Nova Scotia—was formalized under the *British North America Act*. Manitoba and the Northwest Territories (which at the time included the territory of Alberta and Saskatchewan) joined Canada in 1870. British Columbia entered Confederation in 1871 and Prince Edward Island entered in 1873. Newfoundland was the last province to enter Confederation in 1949.

6. Many early treaties reserved lands ("Indian Reserves") for the exclusive use of Indian people. Reserve lands were sometimes lost through squatting or re-surveys, or more often as a result of formal surrenders or expropriations (ICC 1975). There continue to be conflicts over the extent of reserve lands, including claims that treaty obligations with respect to reserve lands were never fulfilled by government. This latter process is known as "Treaty Land Entitlement Claims."

beginning of movement from a hunter/gatherer society to a sedentary society with a mixed economic base.

In 1867 the *British North America Act* gave the Canadian (Federal) Government responsibility for both Indians and the lands reserved for them. The *Indian Act* of 1876 has been described as a mechanism that .. "deprived Indian people of power and kept them locked in a state of dependency" (Canada 1990). It made Indian people virtual wards of the state and prohibited them from leaving their reservation lands, even to hunt or fish, without written permission. The prohibitions in the *Indian Act*, along with numerous other government policies, were designed, at least covertly, to assimilate Indian people[7] (see Hamilton 1995). Despite its assimilation policy, the Government of Canada continued to negotiate treaties throughout previously-unsettled areas of Canada. Treaties were generally timed to precede widespread settlement in a given region, and were sometimes motivated by the discovery of non-renewable resources (e.g., Treaty 11 was signed in 1921 after oil was found at Norman Wells, Northwest Territories—ICC 1975). The Canadian Government dealt with treaties and other Indian claims through the established administrative structures of government, most notably the Department of Indian Affairs (Daniel 1980). In 1939, the Supreme Court of Canada declared the Inuit to be Indians for the purposes of the *British North America Act*. Inuit (and their claims) were therefore a Federal Government responsibility, but were not subject to the provisions of the *Indian Act* (ICC 1975).

Some regions (including large parts of British Columbia and the Northwest Territories) entered Canadian Confederation without the prior signing of treaties with Aboriginal people. However, constitutional documents continued to recognize the concept of Aboriginal rights, and required that these rights be dealt with in the new provinces entering Confederation. Some examples of these documents include:

---

7. Indians were also prohibited from performing religious ceremonies, wearing traditional costumes, and visiting family members on other reserves. They could not sell produce outside a reserve, own a homestead outside a reserve, or purchase labour-saving farm machinery. Indians could not vote in Federal or Provincial elections, use traditional methods for selecting Chiefs, or hold protest meetings. From 1927 to 1951, Indian bands could not engage the assistance of lawyers or raise money to pursue claims against the Crown (see Hamilton 1995). Prohibitions such as those outlined here were obviously demoralizing to Indian people, and led to the deterioration of traditional Aboriginal societies and continuing social problems.

The evolution and status of wildlife co-management in Canada

- The *Rupert's Land and North-Western Territory Order* (1870), which relieved the Hudson's Bay Company of responsibility for Indian claims. These claims were to be "...disposed of by the Canadian Government in communication with the Imperial Government" (Daniel 1980).
- The *Ontario and Quebec Extension Acts* (1912), which required the newly-expanded provinces to recognize and obtain surrenders of the rights of northern Aboriginal peoples (ICC 1975);
- The *Natural Resource Transfer Agreements* (1930), under which the Federal Government transferred responsibility for natural resources to the prairie Provinces (Alberta, Saskatchewan, and Manitoba). These Agreements obliged the provincial governments to make further lands available if required to meet treaty obligations. These agreements also gave Treaty Indians the right to hunt, trap, and fish for food at all seasons of the year on all unoccupied Crown land (Makowecki 1993).

1.2 From assimilation policy to comprehensive claims

The Federal Government pursued its assimilation policy for more than 100 years of Canadian Confederation (see for example, Hamilton 1995, Wavey 1993, Ross 1992). In 1969, the Liberal Government of Pierre Elliott Trudeau issued a *Statement of the Government of Canada on Indian Policy* (also known as the *White Paper on Indian Policy*), which recommended disbanding the Department of Indian Affairs and ending the special status of Indian people. While this policy was consistent with the Liberal philosophy of equality for all citizens, it elicited a strong reaction from Aboriginal organizations (ICC 1975). All across Canada, Aboriginal organizations rallied against the proposed policy, while at the same time articulating their views of Aboriginal rights.[8] Reaction to the *1969 White Paper* was a catalyst for the development and growth of increasingly influential Native organizations (Daniel 1980, Simmons and Netro 1995), and an important factor leading to the development of

---

8. Aboriginal people interpreted the government's intended policy as an end to the special relationship between themselves and the Crown. The 1969 policy, if adopted, would have meant an end to reserves or other Aboriginal territories, an abandonment of existing treaty obligations, and an end to the signing of new Treaties. Many non-Aboriginal Canadians were also outraged by the Government's intended policy (see Hamilton 1995).

government policy on Aboriginal claims. The growth of Aboriginal organizations resulted in documentation of a different perspective on treaties and other aspects of Aboriginal rights. Canada's Aboriginal people regarded treaties as sacred documents with the Crown, and have consistently asserted that the written versions of many treaties differ from the verbal promises made by Agents of the Crown. The Aboriginal view of treaties is as mechanisms for sharing resources with newcomers to traditional territories, not as mechanisms for extinguishing Aboriginal rights in lands or other resources (see Hamilton 1995).

Another important factor in the development of government policy was recognition of Aboriginal rights by the legal system. While some of the more draconian provisions of the *Indian Act* had been overturned, the concept of Aboriginal rights did not receive widespread recognition within the legal system until 1973. Elias (1989:3) summarizes the legal status of Aboriginal rights in Canada from 1887 to 1973:

"It had been decided that Aboriginal title was not based on ancient traditions of possession or the common law, but upon an act of the Crown; rights to self-government were not acknowledged; the exercise of Aboriginal rights was subject to federal and provincial regulation; extinguishment of rights could be unilaterally effected at the will of the Crown, and consent was not necessary".

A 1973 court case, known as the "Calder Case" (*Calder vs. Attorney-General of British Columbia*), marked the beginning of a new era of government policy. This case involved the Nisga'a Indians of British Columbia, who were seeking a ruling that their Aboriginal title had never been extinguished. The Nisga'a lost their case in the Supreme Court of Canada in a 4-3 decision. However, three of the judges acknowledged continued Aboriginal rights based on occupation (ICC 1975). The Calder Case influenced subsequent government policy and is widely recognized as the basis for modern treaty-making with Aboriginal people (see for example, Simmons and Netro 1995, Hamilton 1995, Notzke 1994, Bailey *et al.* 1995, ICC 1975). The Calder Case had an immediate impact on government policy, and in August 1973, the Federal Government unveiled a new policy for negotiation of "land claims," under which the government was prepared to negotiate compensation for Native peoples in return for their traditional interests in lands[9] (Hamilton 1995). The 1973 "land claims" policy referred to the *Royal Proclamation of 1763* and recognized the loss of traditional use and occupancy of lands, as well as loss of a way of life (ICC 1975). It must be noted that acceptance of the Calder Case as a foundation for this policy is by no means universal (see for example, Smith 1995); nonetheless, the Government of Canada has concluded numerous comprehensive claims settlements with Aboriginal groups under the 1973 and subsequent "land claims" policies.

Third-party interests have also played a role in the settlement of comprehensive claims in Canada. As in earlier periods of Canadian history, resolution of Aboriginal interests was a necessary precursor to northern development. Specific interest in the oil and gas resources of the Arctic, particularly in the Beaufort Sea, was a key motivator for the settlement of some comprehensive claims (see Doubleday 1989). One of the objectives of the Federal Government's 1987 "Comprehensive Land Claims Policy" was to provide certainty and clarity of rights to ownership and use of lands and resources. The Government intended that the final settlement of comprehensive claims would "...result in certainty and predictability with respect to the use and disposition of lands affected by the settlements" (Canada 1986:9). It should be noted that large parts of Canada are not subject to the comprehensive claims process, since these areas are already covered by earlier treaties. In these areas, the resolution of Aboriginal interests in lands and resources is an ongoing process. The courts often play an important role in the resolution of conflicts arising from this process.

1.3 Comprehensive claims and co-management of natural resources

The *James Bay and Northern Quebec Agreement* (JBNQA) of 1975 was the first comprehensive claim in Canada. Negotiations leading to this agreement began before the 1973 "land claims" policy, when a

---

9. The government's 1973 policy established two types of "claims". Comprehensive claims focused on previously unsettled, unceded, and unsurrendered Aboriginal title to lands and resources. Specific claims focused on compensation for breaches of past treaties or loss of land through Federal mismanagement (Hamilton 1995). Specific claims have in some cases resulted in reimbursement of Indian bands for land lost through fraudulent surrenders (Notzke 1994). Comprehensive claims have resulted in the establishment of wildlife co-management regimes which include legislated access to both wildlife resources and shared decision-making.

commission appointed by the Quebec Government found that the Province had not honoured the provisions of its 1912 *Boundary Extension Act* (see Section 1.1). Quebec's intention to develop the hydroelectric resources of James Bay lent some urgency to the settlement of this claim. In 1973, the James Bay Cree and the Northern Quebec Inuit obtained an injunction from the Quebec Superior Court, ordering a halt to the James Bay hydro-electric project. The court agreed that the Province could not "... develop or otherwise open up these lands for settlement without ... the prior agreement of the Indians and Eskimo" (ICC 1975:30). Although the injunction was eventually overturned by a higher court, an Agreement was negotiated between the James Bay Cree, the Inuit of Quebec, the Province of Quebec, and the Government of Canada.

The JBNQA included ownership of lands, monetary compensation, and exclusive hunting and trapping rights. The *Agreement* also gave the Cree and Inuit an equal share in wildlife management throughout the entire area covered by the *Agreement*, which included considerable Crown land. This equal share in resource management decision-making was a "...significant departure from traditional forms of wildlife management elsewhere in Canada" (MacLachlan 1994). The JBNQA set the tone for future comprehensive claims in Canada, all of which include some form of co-management of wildlife and other natural resources. Co-management through comprehensive claims usually involves establishment of one or more committees comprising equal numbers of government and Aboriginal representatives.[10] Although in theory these committees are advisory to government, in practice they are *de facto* decision-making bodies[11] (Swerdfager 1992).

Co-management of wildlife in Canada has also developed outside the comprehensive claims process, often in response to a real or

---

10. The role and composition of co-management boards varies, depending on the specific terms of each comprehensive claim. For example, under the *Nunavut Agreement* (covering the eastern and central Arctic), government members of co-management boards represent the public. Under the *Inuvialuit Final Agreement* (covering the western Arctic), government members represent their governments.

11. Wildlife co-management boards operate within the framework of Ministerial government based on the British parliamentary system. Government Ministers cannot completely delegate their authority to co-management boards, and are ultimately responsible for ensuring that the principles of conservation are upheld (see Swerdfager 1992). Ministers retain a veto power, which they may exercise in the interests of conservation or public safety (see Introduction to this report).

The evolution and status of wildlife co-management in Canada

perceived crisis in wildlife management [12] (Swerdfager 1992). Numerous single-species co-management initiatives have emerged when conventional government approaches have proved inadequate to deal with a decline in wildlife numbers. A classic example of this type of *ad hoc* wildlife co-management is the Beverly-Qamanirjuaq[13] Caribou Management Board (BQCMB), one of the earliest examples in North America. The BQCMB was established in 1982 in response to a widely perceived crisis in management of the Beverly and Qamanirjuaq herds of barren-ground caribou. This board comprises 13 members:

- five members represent the governments of Canada, NWT, Manitoba, and Saskatchewan;
- eight members represent the 18 Aboriginal communities that border on the caribou range[14] and use the caribou.

This board is frequently cited as a successful example of wildlife co-management involving multiple stakeholders, and is arguably the most successful case of co-management in Canada (Berkes and Henley 1997). Osherenko (1988) points out that the Board's use of English as a working language has limited the inclusion of traditional ecological knowledge (TEK). In spite of this, the BQCMB has indeed been quite successful. This success is based partly on the Board not having been

---

12. These *ad hoc* co-management boards usually deal with single species of wildlife, typically species important for subsistence such as moose, caribou, and bison. *Ad-hoc* co-management boards are not part of the comprehensive claims process and do not have the same legislative basis.

13. '*Qamanirjuaq*' and 'Kaminuriak' are alternate spellings referring to a lake located on the calving ground of this herd of barren-ground caribou. 'Kaminuriak' is the anglicized version used in older documents, while '*Qamanirjuaq*' is the Aboriginal spelling for this location.

14. The Beverly and Qamanirjuaq barren-ground caribou herds range along the western coast of Hudson Bay, northern Manitoba, northern Saskatchewan, and southwestern Nunavut.

tested by a 'crisis of scarcity,'[15] and partly on its consensus approach to decision-making (see Usher 1991, 1993).

Co-management of wildlife through comprehensive claims and other *ad hoc* means can be seen as part of a larger shift in wildlife policy in North America, as wildlife management moved away from the biological approach which characterized the three decades ending in 1969 (Picton 1991). Starting in the early 1970s, there was increasing recognition by governments, Aboriginal groups, academics, and others, of the need to reconcile the 'two solitudes' of government (state) and local (community-based) management (see Berkes 1994). Many writings on sharing wildlife management (e.g., Usher 1986, Swerdfager 1992) focus on conflicts between state and community-based management systems and potential benefits of cooperation.

Osherenko (1988:41) argues that co-management is necessary for efficient and equitable management of wildlife:

> *Government agencies cannot implement and enforce their regulations without Native cooperation, and natives cannot protect the resources or guarantee access to those resources without the cooperation of government agencies.*

Usher (1991:21) confirms this sentiment:

> *The positive approach for governments would be to give recognition and force to aboriginal systems of tenure, management, harvesting, and utilization, by entering into co-management or self-government arrangements. The alternative is to engage in long and costly skirmishes in court, which aboriginal people would appear to have a good chance of winning, on the facts.*

Government response to the concept of wildlife co-management has not been uniform across Canada (see Section 1.4). In the northern

---

15. Both the perceived decline and subsequent increase in population estimates for this herd were based on scientific survey data. The increasing numbers of caribou detected in surveys were attributed to factors such as refinements in survey techniques and improvements in the available information base. It became apparent that "... as native users had claimed from the start, low populations at the southern end of the winter range did not indicate precipitous declines in total herd sizes..." (Osherenko 1988). Restrictions on hunting were under consideration but were not implemented.

The evolution and status of wildlife co-management in Canada

territories, where comprehensive claims are the rule rather than the exception, government has been receptive. In the more southerly Provinces, comprehensive claims are the exception rather than the rule, and government response has been more varied. Co-management of wildlife in the Canadian Provinces is often coloured by complex Federal/Provincial/Aboriginal relations. The (Provincial) Government of British Columbia, for example, has only recently acknowledged any validity to comprehensive claims (Notzke 1994). This acknowledgement is likely a response to recent decisions by the Supreme Court of Canada. Determination of current Aboriginal rights to wildlife (and other natural resources) in Canada has been relegated to the Supreme Court of Canada. Canada's highest court also plays a major role in determining the relationship between Aboriginal people and Provincial governments. Government policy has evolved in this context. Current Federal policy has generally attempted to keep one step ahead of the Court, while Provincial policy has tended to lag one or more steps behind.

Section 35.1 of the *Canadian Constitution Act* (1982) recognizes and affirms the existing Aboriginal and Treaty rights of the Aboriginal peoples of Canada. Thus, Aboriginal rights in a comprehensive claims settlement are protected not only by legislation implementing that claim settlement, but also by the Canadian Constitution. In a landmark 1990 decision, the "Sparrow Case" (Regina *vs.* Sparrow), the Supreme Court ruled that Indian Treaty rights to fish for food could not be infringed or abrogated unless justification was shown. The Court further noted that these fishing rights were to be given priority over other fishing rights [16] (see Makowecki 1993). In 1993, the Court ruled that the principles adopted in the "Sparrow Case" apply to wildlife as well as fish (Regina *vs.* Dick, Notzke 1994). Recent Canadian case law suggests that Aboriginal people have constitutionally protected resource-use rights which include a first priority harvest as well as a stake in the conservation and allocation of the resources in question (Haugh 1994). Not all recent court decisions have been supportive of Aboriginal and Treaty rights (see Notzke 1994), but in general there has been increasing recognition of these rights by the Canadian legal system.

---

16. It is not implied that there has been smooth adoption of this ruling in policy or practice. There continue to be many conflicts related to implementation of this and related rulings by the Supreme Court.

1.4 The current status of wildlife co-management in Canada

Co-management is a continuing and probably irreversible development in Canadian wildlife management. Co-management through comprehensive claims is now the dominant management regime for wildlife in Canada's northern territories (Yukon, NWT, and Nunavut) (see Roberts 1995). In the Canadian provinces, co-management through comprehensive claims is rare, and co-management of wildlife through a variety of *ad-hoc* means is not consistently applied. Some provinces have more than two decades of involvement in co-management, while others have virtually none. Keith (1993) commented that co-management is not the case for most Indian and Métis people in Canada and this statement is probably still true. This statement is not true for Canadian Inuit.

Murray (1995: i) summarized the status of co-management practice in Canada as follows:

> *Not all jurisdictions have the same understanding of the term; the amount of shared decision-making power and authority varies widely; ... co-management may occur between a jurisdiction and a single group of stakeholders, all of whom are Aboriginal, as well as between a jurisdiction and many different stakeholders, few of whom are Aboriginal.*

In 1993, Makowecki reported that four provinces (out of ten) were using co-management in their relationships with Aboriginal peoples regarding hunting, fishing, and trapping. In 1995, Murray reported that five provinces had shared decision-making arrangements for environmental and resource management. At least two other provinces have experimented with forms of co-management since 1995. There is evidence to indicate increasing interest and involvement in wildlife co-management in the Canadian provinces. Co-management of wildlife in the provinces will continue to be affected by complex political factors. Makowecki (1993) described the relationships of government wildlife agencies to Aboriginal groups as "...fluid, rapidly evolving and occasionally confused." This is a fitting description of the current status of wildlife co-management outside the comprehensive claims process.

Wildlife co-management through comprehensive claims continues to expand throughout Canada's northern territories. As of 1995, a total of ten comprehensive land claims had been finalized (Smith 1995):

The evolution and status of wildlife co-management in Canada

1. The *James Bay and Northern Quebec Agreement* in northern Quebec (1975)
2. The *Northeastern Quebec Agreement* with the Napaski Indian Band (1978)
3. The *Inuvialuit Final Agreement* with the Inuit of the western Arctic (1984)
4. The *Gwich'in Agreement* with the Gwich'in (Indians) of the Mackenzie River Delta, NWT (1992)
5. The *Nunavut Agreement* with the Inuit of the eastern and central Arctic (1993)
6. The *Sahtu Dene and Métis Agreement* with the Great Bear Lake region of the NWT (1993)
7. The *Vuntut Gwichin Agreement* in the Yukon (1994)
8. The *Nacho Nyak Dun Agreement* in the Yukon (1994)
9. The *Champagne and Aishihik Agreement* in the Yukon (1994)
10. The *Teslin Tlingit Agreement* in the Yukon (1994)

The Nisga'a Treaty, signed in August 1998, was the first comprehensive claim in the Province of British Columbia; wildlife co-management within the context of comprehensive claims therefore can be expected to expand to those areas of Canada in which comprehensive claims have not been finalized.

Much of Canadian experience with wildlife co-management has yet to be subject to extensive evaluation. Nonetheless, a growing body of literature indicates that co-management of wildlife has been successful in many respects, particularly in overcoming conflicts between Aboriginal and state systems of wildlife management (Osherenko 1988). Co-management also greatly enhances the collection and exchange of information on wildlife resources (Swerdfager 1992). Pinkerton (1989) discusses potential resource management functions of co-management in the context of local fisheries. These functions apply to wildlife as well, and include data gathering and analysis and harvest allocation and regulation. Bailey *et al.* (1995) describe the benefits of wildlife co-management in the context of a comprehensive claim, the *Inuvialuit Final Agreement* (IFA) of 1984.

One of the most important benefits is overcoming a mutual mistrust between resource harvesters and government representatives. This mistrust has characterized many past interactions between the state system and Aboriginal peoples, as explained by Swerdfager (1992:19):

> *"... respect for other parties' management expertise and knowledge is not a platitude but of critical importance to the success [of co-management]. The state system has not usually*

acknowledged the management values of Aboriginal knowledge and customs, while Aboriginal peoples have tended to distrust the state system."

Major progress has been achieved in terms of increased respect and understanding between the parties involved in wildlife co-management; however, this issue remains as a key challenge for the future (see Usher 1993).

Current issues in wildlife co-management in Canada are numerous and include the following:

- Overcoming cultural and institutional barriers to implementation of co-management arrangements.
- Building relationships between Aboriginal communities and other stakeholders, particularly at the provincial level.
- Achieving consensus on conservation principles. This issue is particularly important in the context of comprehensive claims, where 'conservation' may have different meanings to Aboriginal and non-Aboriginal members of co-management boards, or to co-management boards and governments.
- Determining the relationship between co-management and Aboriginal self-government. There are many views on this subject, ranging from co-management as a vehicle for empowerment of Aboriginal communities, to co-management as another assimilation policy.
- Achieving equality of partnerships in co-management. Co-management implies equality of participants, but government and Aboriginal members of co-management boards rarely have equal access to resources to support their participation in the process.
- Determining the role of the public and other (non-government, non-Aboriginal) stakeholders in co-management. This is an important issue in some comprehensive claims, where there is no formal representation of the general public or of other stakeholders, such as industry.
- Paying the costs associated with co-management. There has been little documentation of the costs associated with co-management, or evaluation of its cost-effectiveness. This is an emerging issue in times of fiscal restraint since, to date, most of the costs of co-management have been borne by government.
- Identification of conditions under which co-management is not appropriate. The majority of co-management literature focuses on positive aspects of the practice. There may be situations where co-

management is not the best vehicle for achieving wildlife management and/or community development objectives.

A number of recent summaries (including Makowecki 1993; Murray 1995; Roberts 1995, 1996), include discussions of these and other current issues from the perspectives of regulatory agencies and Aboriginal people.

1.4.1 Traditional ecological knowledge

One of the most difficult and controversial issues in Canadian wildlife co-management is use of traditional ecological knowledge (TEK) of Aboriginal people. This issue is highlighted because it is topical and it illustrates some of the practical difficulties encountered in melding the state and community-based systems of wildlife management. In theory, wildlife co-management represents an opportunity to combine the diachronic knowledge of Aboriginal people with the synchronic knowledge of western science, resulting in improved understanding and better decision-making (see Freeman and Carbyn 1988).

In practice, use of TEK has received little attention in policy circles, and few jurisdictions in Canada have policies related to TEK. The NWT policy, which recognizes TEK as a valid and essential source of information, was recently applied in the assessment of the environmental and socio-economic impacts of a proposed development project. The proponent was directed to give full and equal consideration to traditional knowledge and scientific research in the assessment of potential impacts. Many practical difficulties were encountered in attempting to apply this policy,[17] leading to some heated and highly polarized debates (see Stevenson 1997; Berkes and Henley 1997; Howard and Widdowson 1996, 1997). One of the key points raised in this debate was the cultural context of TEK, and the difficulty in applying this knowledge in other contexts. Context is an essential issue in the use of TEK, given that the context for North American 'wildlife management' (including co-management) is western science. There are few indications that western science is about to undergo a fundamental restructuring to accommodate the 'full and equal' consideration of traditional knowledge, either in wildlife management or in other fields (such as medicine).

---

17. These difficulties included coming to agreement on the definition of TEK, obtaining access to this knowledge in a usable form, and dealing with intellectual property rights related to TEK.

In the context of western science, some TEK has been and is being incorporated in Canadian wildlife co-management decision-making. Wildlife biologists have utilized TEK in their research for many years and recognize that science "...is only part of the answer" (see Stirling 1990). In some cases, similar conclusions have been drawn using western science and Aboriginal TEK, and these cases offer the best prospects for melding the two systems. Situations where western science and TEK lead to contradictory conclusions represent major difficulties for the wildlife co-management process, and one of the prime challenges for the future.

1.5 The future of wildlife co-management in Canada

In Canada's northern territories, co-management through comprehensive claims is becoming established as the dominant system for wildlife management, and this arrangement can be expected to continue into the future. In the context of comprehensive claims, some of Canada's Aboriginal people are recognizing the potential for wildlife co-management to provide career opportunities within their communities, and are seeking appropriate training for participation in this field. More government jurisdictions are examining co-management, and in the future there will be more discussion of this topic in policy circles. There will also be more documentation and evaluation of Canadian wildlife co-management experience.

In Canada's southern provinces (outside of the comprehensive claims process), co-management of wildlife is not yet well established. Implementation of co-management in the provincial context faces many hurdles and is subject to complex political factors. At the same time, the co-management process offers prospects for resolution of complex resource management issues as well as opportunities for building relationships between stakeholders. Co-management is not a panacea, however, and at this time it is not clear whether this process is the way of the future for wildlife management in the Canadian provinces. It is clear that cooperative management, either through co-management or other means, will be essential to ensure the future sustainability of wildlife populations and habitats in northern Canada.

CHAPTER 2:

Subsistence hunting of wildlife in the Canadian north

Mina Berkes and Fikret Berkes

The importance of community-based wildlife management can be interpreted in terms of the needs of local groups to conserve resources which they use. The higher the degree of dependence, the more important the need for successful local management. In this regard, ancient subsistence hunting systems provide a striking case: survival was the ultimate criterion of successful community-based wildlife management. Today, subsistence is seen as critical to cultural survival and maintenance of a distinctive and valued identity (Freeman *et al.* 1992).

In North America, there is a long tradition of hunting for food by Aboriginal groups. Since the 1970s in Canada, this tradition has included hunting to supply fur trade posts, exploration parties, and other aspects of European settlement. During this earlier period, Aboriginal hunting was carried out under its own rules, with the exception of certain rules for beaver trapping introduced by the Hudson's Bay Company around 1820 (Brightman 1993). In southern Canada, many of the hunting areas of Aboriginal groups were transformed into agricultural areas occupied by Euro-Canadians as the land was settled throughout the 1700s and the 1800s. Northern Aboriginal groups were encouraged to settle in permanent communities, but were not displaced or assimilated to any great extent, and their hunting traditions continued. In northern Canada, government regulations had relatively little effect on Aboriginal subsistence hunting until perhaps the 1940s and the 1950s. In the 1960s and 1970s, northern development projects and the incursion of recreational hunters into the north led to conflicts over wildlife use, with the result that subsistence hunting came under increasing government regulation.

This chapter provides an overview of northern Canadian Aboriginal land use and subsistence resource management, including social and cultural aspects. Using the example of the James Bay Cree of northern Ontario, this chapter discusses subsistence hunting as a vital part of the northern mixed economy, and comments on subsistence as a land use option for the future. The dictionary definition of the term subsistence as "what one lives on" accurately describes Aboriginal use of wildlife resources in northern Canada. We use the term *subsistence* not merely as an economic concept but as one that denotes important societal relationships and cultural characteristics in indigenous societies (Freeman 1993). The term *harvesting*, which describes the activity of subsistence, refers collectively to "all hunting, fishing, trapping, and gathering." The term *subsistence economy* indicates "non-market values of goods and services from the land." *Traditional economy*, used interchangeably with *land-based sector*, denotes "subsistence plus fur and fish production." *Land use* refers to "activities pertaining to harvesting wildlife and other wild products"; it includes transportation routes and campsites, as well as culturally significant areas.

2.1 Historical context

There has been a widespread assumption that historically, Aboriginal groups did not manage resources, as populations of hunters were considered too small to have had an impact on wildlife resources. While this may have been true in some sparsely populated areas such as the Churchill River basin in the central Canadian subarctic (Brightman 1993), there is evidence elsewhere that community-based management systems did exist, and that Aboriginal wildlife hunters did have concepts of sustainability. A case in point is the subsistence hunt of geese in James Bay. Barnston (1861) was one of the first biologists/naturalists to attempt an estimate of wild goose populations in North America. Based on a field survey indicating that the Cree Indians of James Bay killed some 74,000 geese per year, and an elders' rule of thumb that "for every goose killed, 20 must leave the Bay", Barnston came up with a total goose population estimate of 1,200,000. This is an entirely plausible figure, and well within modern population estimates which give a range of one to two million Canada geese (*Branta canadensis*), and lesser snow geese (*Anser caerulescens*) that use James Bay as a flyway.

The use of territories provides further evidence of Aboriginal wildlife management. Speck (1915) saw the system of hunting territories used by the Aboriginal people of Labrador as a method of resource conservation. His findings were later attacked on the basis that family-based hunting territories came into being after the fur trade, and therefore could not have represented an Aboriginal land tenure system. Although the latter argument about the origin of the family territory system is probably correct, the point is still being debated (Bishop and Morantz 1986), and from a resource management point of view, Speck's original point is valid.

Community-based (but not family-based) territories were probably the primary practice for resource management at one time in Canada. While land tenure systems varied among wildlife species, areas, and cultures, most Aboriginal groups had rules for controlling access of outsiders to wildlife resources, and for allocating resources within their groups. Historically, such resource tenure systems with community-based rules were common, not only in North America, but throughout the world, and not only with wildlife, but with many kinds of living resources.

2.2 Land use and resource management

While most Aboriginal land tenure systems in North America have disappeared, some in the Canadian north are still functional. However, the pattern of Aboriginal land use has changed. Historically, many Aboriginal societies moved seasonally between hunting and fishing areas, but now almost all hunters live for most of the year in permanent communities, and travel from these communities to harvesting areas. This contemporary land use pattern is the outcome of a government policy of settling indigenous populations into centralized communities, a policy motivated in part by the belief that a land-based economy was not viable, and that indigenous peoples should be integrated into the modern wage economy. However, wage opportunities are scarce in remote northern communities, and large development projects have not proved to be significant providers of jobs for Aboriginal people. Even when they are located far from wildlife, Aboriginal communities in the Canadian north have continued to sustain themselves by channelling cash from transfer payments and wage employment into mechanized transportation to enable access to traditional resources.

Since the 1970s, much detailed work has been carried out on the territorial land tenure systems of the James Bay Cree (Feit 1991). These systems are of the communal property type. Each community holds a communal territory which is further subdivided into hunting territories of family groups. A senior hunter leads each group and enforces the community's rules. Only members of the family or people invited by them are permitted to trap furs on this land, but it is generally understood that any community member can hunt or fish to feed his/her family. Within a territory, individual hunters lay claim to beaver houses. Violations of general rules of hunting, fishing, and trapping are dealt with under customary law and enforced by social sanction.

Hunting rights limit the number of hunters who can operate in the family territories and in the communal territory as a whole. High levels of wildlife productivity are therefore maintained by limiting hunting pressure. Where the (human) population is large and growing, can these territorial systems limit the number of active hunters and stabilize the overall hunting pressure? We examined this question using an 18-year data set from the eastern James Bay area. Over this time period, the regional Cree population nearly doubled, but the size of the population participating (i.e., the number of active hunters) in fact remained stable, as did the resource base (Berkes and Fast 1996).

The extent and persistence of Aboriginal land use in the Canadian north have been recognized only relatively recently. The pioneering study which provided inspiration and methodology for many subsequent ones was *The Inuit Land Use and Occupancy Project* (Freeman 1976). Composite maps, combining those for different resources and for different time periods, showed that the Inuit used almost all of the Arctic—a land that southerners had always considered 'empty'. Riewe's (1992) *Nunavut Atlas* continued this work and provided a comprehensive series of land use maps that were used in land selection by the Inuit as part of a comprehensive settlement, the *Nunavut Agreement* of 1993. This *Agreement* resulted in the creation of a self-governing Inuit territory, Nunavut, in the Canadian eastern and central Arctic in 1999.

Many Aboriginal land use studies go beyond the utilitarian function of documenting Native occupancy of land or the impacts of development. They also document the meaning of land and 'homeland' for groups of Aboriginal people. Land use maps can be used to convey aspects of Aboriginal cultures and traditional ecological knowledge. For example, Brody's (1981) work shows the feasibility of achieving cross-cultural insights using maps as a focus of contact between the Aboriginal and non-Aboriginal worlds. Culture consists of a storehouse of knowledge for a people to guide their relationships and activities within their environment. This knowledge is guided by a world view or a mental 'map' of relationships of a people to places, people, and animals. Places are very important for cultural identity, as in the *-miut* (the people of -) groups of the Inuit. Many Aboriginal groups and subgroups defined their identify, as the Inuit do, in terms of the places in which they hunt, gather, live, and travel through the annual cycle.

2.3 Social and cultural aspects of subsistence hunting

Land use and subsistence are important for social and cultural reasons, including:
- education of the young and transmission of knowledge (Ohmagari and Berkes 1997);
- perpetuation of social values, such as sharing and reciprocity (Freeman 1993);
- reproduction of culture, which is unconsciously known and embodied in action (Preston 1975).

Among many Canadian Aboriginal groups, hunting is not merely use of animals and the environment to obtain food, it is a religious activity (Tanner 1979). Speck (1935:72) expressed this relationship many decades ago:

> *"To the Montagnais-Naskapi ... the animals of the forest, the tundra, and the waters of the interior and the coast exist in a specific relation. They have become the objects of engrossing magico-religious activity, for to them hunting is a holy occupation."*

Even among contemporary hunters in northern Manitoba, long acculturated and converted to Christianity, hunting continues as a spiritual activity in which "you got to keep it holy" (Brightman 1993). Making a livelihood from the land sustains the distinctive cultural ideology of the group, as well as the very important social relationships within the group. It helps maintain social identity and provides a source of values. Social relations of cooperation, sharing, gift-giving, gender-role maintenance, and reciprocity (with both humans and animals) are part of the larger meaning of subsistence. Knowledge, values, and identity are transferred to succeeding generations through the annual, cyclical repetition of livelihood activities based on traditional ecological knowledge (Freeman 1993).

One example of the relationship between subsistence hunting and social organization is provided by the Dene (northern Athapascans) who occupy the subarctic zone of northern Canada from Manitoba to the Alaska border. Dene social organization can be explained in terms of adaptation to caribou movements. Rules regarding kinship and marriage favoured the formation of social links across a broad front, thus providing a communications network extending through groups dependent on the caribou.

> *"Hunting groups were strategically situated in a long narrow front (of some 1,000 km), with relatively shallow depth, near the treeline ... They were thus potentially in contact with all the constituent herds of the Kaminuriak, Beverly, and Bathurst populations of caribou. The hunting groups may be viewed as strategically situated reconnaissance patrols for collecting information on caribou movements and intentions... Survival resulted from the spatial placement of regional and local bands and hunting groups, bound to one another by complex ties of kinship and marriage."* (Smith 1978)

The spatial arrangement of the Dene bands followed the transition zone from forest to tundra, making it possible for the hunters to exploit either zone. Local band centres were located at fishing lakes to provide a reliable food supply. Summer excursions to the north of the treeline kept the Dene well informed of caribou distributions. According to the archaeological record, this spatial arrangement had considerable time depth, allowing hunters to accumulate many generations of data (Smith 1978).

Even in recent years, the social and cultural value of bush food consumption has continued to be important for Canadian Aboriginal groups. Aboriginal identity is partly defined in terms of having access to and consuming bush food. Wildlife as food is important for core cultural values, such as sharing. The distribution of subsistence harvests to relatives and neighbours remains a widespread practice in northern Canada. For example, among the western James Bay Cree, about 50 per cent of all respondents reported sharing their food with three or more other families. Even in the relatively large communities of Moose Factory and Attawapiskat (Ontario), sharing with more than six families was common (Berkes *et al.* 1994).

2.4 Subsistence hunting as a vital part of the northern mixed economy

The persistence of Aboriginal land use parallels the persistence of a traditional economy in northern Canada. This land-based economy has remained a cornerstone of the mixed economy of many communities in the northern parts of the provinces and the northern territories. Despite the predictions of economic planners to the contrary, the land-based economy has not been replaced by the modern wage economy (George and Preston 1987). However, much of the value of the traditional economy has remained 'invisible' to conventional economic analysis.

Subsistence hunting of wildlife in the Canadian North

Hunting brings food to the table but results in little cash transaction in the economy. Since the products of hunting do not pass through the market, government statistics have not placed any value on subsistence, and hunters have been technically defined as 'unemployed'. Today, subsistence hunting is increasingly recognized as important for the economy of small northern Canadian communities. The Government of the Northwest Territories (GNWT), for example, has policies and programmes to support subsistence harvesting and its role in community economic development.

In the NWT, Usher (1989) estimated that subsistence production and processing added about 10 percent to total labour income. An estimated 80 percent of Native households participated in the domestic economy, for a total of 4,000 Native households and 5,500 active harvesters. As well, several thousand women prepared the meat for consumption. Despite the fact that harvesting was done on a part-time basis, Usher (1989) estimated that the average Arctic hunter took 1,000 kg to 1,500 kg of meat and fish annually with an inputed value of $10,000 to $15,000 (Cdn.). Inputed values are calculated using the Berger Commission (Mackenzie Valley Pipeline Inquiry) approach, in which the harvest of bush meat can be converted into cash equivalents by using replacement values (Berger 1977). Using this method, the value of bush meat is converted into dollar equivalents by calculating the cost of a comparable kind of meat in the local store. For example, harvested waterfowl is valued by comparing it to the local store cost of chicken; big and small game is compared to local red meat prices, and so on.

Table 2.1 provides an example of a subsistence harvesting survey and calculation of inputed values based on replacement value of bush meat. The potential edible weight of 106kg/yr per capita in this study was obtained by dividing the total harvest (686,500 kg per year) by the resident Aboriginal population in the year (6,475). This finding may be compared to several other values in the literature, as compiled and standardized by Berkes and Fast (1996). In the Keewatin Region of the NWT, the 1984-85 harvest was estimated at 895,298 kg of wild food for 3,999 Inuit, for a per capita value of 224 kg/yr. In northern Quebec, an Inuit harvest of 1,100,179 kg was estimated for a population of 3,857, giving a per capita value of 285 kg/yr. In eastern James Bay, harvest by Cree Indians was estimated at 809,101 kg for 7,022 people in 1978-79, for a per capita value of 115 kg/yr. The general finding is that many Inuit communities in the Canadian Arctic obtain in the order of 200 kg per person per year of bush food, mostly from wildlife (including waterfowl and marine mammals) and some from fish. Various Indian groups living in the subarctic zone of Canada, who are not as isolated from southern Canada as are the Inuit, harvest on the order of 100 kg per person per year (Berkes and Fast 1996).

Table 2.1 Subsistence harvest of eight western James Bay Cree communities (total population 6,475) in 1990; showing potential edible weights by species group and their replacement values.

Species Group*	Edible Weights (kg)	Replacement Value (1990 Canadian $)
Waterfowl	242,000.00	2,360,500.00
Fish	134,000.00	1,724,500.00
Fur animals	25,000.00	289,900.00
Big Game	256,500.00	3,128,000.00
Small Game	29,000.00	344,000.00
Total	**686,500.00**	**7,846,900.00**

* **Note:** 'Waterfowl' includes two major goose species and several duck species; beaver is the major fur animal; moose is the major big game species, followed by caribou; small game includes snowshoe hare, several species of grouse, and ptarmigan. Source: Berkes *et al.* 1994.

Returning to Table 2.1, the replacement value or income-in-kind from bush food is substantial in small, semi-isolated Aboriginal communities where the official unemployment rate is typically above 50 percent. On a per household basis, the average yearly value of the subsistence harvest for the western James Bay Cree (1,116 households) was estimated at $7,030. Adjusted to constant 1991 dollars, many of the values in the Arctic were in the order of $15,000–$17,000 per household per year, and those in the subarctic were in the order of $6,000 - $9,000 (Berkes and Fast 1996). If other subsistence products, such as fuelwood, berries, medicinal plants and fur are similarly valued, the in-kind income per household increases—in the case of the western James Bay study, to $8,400 per year (Berkes *et al.* 1994).

A number of studies have included data on both the traditional and the non-traditional economy, including wage income and transfer payments, making it possible to calculate the relative value of bush meat and other subsistence products in the overall economy. The relative value of the traditional economy was as follows:

Subsistence hunting of wildlife in the Canadian North

- 58 percent of the total economy in Sanikiluaq, NWT;
- 35 percent in Pinehouse Lake, northern Saskatchewan; half of this from commercial fisheries;
- 27 percent in Waswanipi, northern Quebec;
- 25 percent in western James Bay, northern Ontario;
- 22 percent in the eastern James Bay region, northern Quebec;
- 11 percent, excluding land-based commodities, in northern Manitoba (summarized by Berkes *et al.* 1994).

The above data may be considered indicative of the quantitative significance of the subsistence economy, but they should be treated with caution. All of them are based largely on questionnaire studies and are subject to the various limitations of such studies (Usher and Wenzel 1987). Despite these limitations, however, the major conclusion is that the traditional economy of indigenous groups, such as the western James Bay Cree, has remained alive and quantitatively significant. The value represented by bush meat ($8,400 per household per year and $9.4 million for the region), is in the order of one-third as large as the entire cash economy, easily exceeding the income from any other single source. It should be noted that harvest studies to determine subsistence needs are a requirement of the northern comprehensive claim settlements. These and other studies can be expected to provide more information on the importance of subsistence activities in the economy of Canada's northern communities.

2.5 Subsistence as a future land use option

The major produce of the land in the Canadian north is wildlife and fish protein, and Aboriginal people have utilized this renewable resource base for millennia. However, due to increasing pressures from development projects, improved access and expanding human populations, it may become more and more difficult to continue using animal resources within their rates of renewability. In view of the continued importance of the traditional economy, many indigenous groups have asked for a more active role in resource management (see for example, RCAP 1996). Historically, most wildlife harvests were from Crown lands over which Aboriginal groups had no recognized jurisdiction. Many Aboriginal groups have pursued land claims as a means of securing a role in the management of wildlife and other renewable resources.

Even in areas with settled comprehensive claims, there continues to be tension and conflict between community-based resource management and government management. Differences are to some extent cultural and philosophical, but they also concern the question of land and resource claims, and involve the all-important issue of property rights—the question of who owns the resources. Wildlife, lands, and waters used by Aboriginal peoples were, and in many cases still are, non-exclusive resources and communal property. Sustainable use of these resources requires collective decision-making and enforcement of agreed-upon rules among community members. Among Aboriginal people, the traditional values of community, social obligations, respect, reciprocity, and consensus decision-making may be seen as adaptations that have survival value in societies dependent on common-property resources.

Canadian law, however, does not recognize the right of ownership to any wild animal until it is killed or captured. In effect, what is viewed as communal property by Aboriginal groups is viewed as state property by government managers, and often as open-access (or a free-for-all) by powerful outside interests. Aboriginal groups, many of whom have been dispossessed over the years by the intrusion of outsiders, take little comfort in the principle that wildlife resources are managed by the state on behalf of all citizens.

> "Only 20 years ago, Canadian governments considered their authority in respect of lands and resources as unlimited, except by signed Treaties, and then only in the most minimal way. The origins of co-management, therefore, were in crisis and struggle... Many people—not only Aboriginal people—have been raising concerns about real or perceived resource depletion and are demanding a share in management decisions." (RCAP 1996:666)

In this context, the significance of community-based management through co-management or other shared decision-making can be appreciated as a mechanism for implementing Aboriginal self-government.

Control over wildlife resources has become a symbol of self-government for many Aboriginal groups, as well as a strategy for social and cultural revitalization movements. In the 1970s, the Berger Commission helped publicize Aboriginal views of the land and the importance of the traditional economy, and contributed to the development of a revitalization and empowerment movement in the Mackenzie Valley (NWT). This issue is in part cultural because hunting is so important for the maintenance of Aboriginal cultures. The loss of subsistence hunting practices deprives indigenous peoples of experiences through which culture can be transmitted. Among the Cree,

Subsistence hunting of wildlife in the Canadian North

for example, the young learn by doing. Cree culture taught on the land includes not only bush skills, but also ethics and values, such as the importance of sharing and reciprocity (Ohmagari and Berkes 1997). Thus, it is of great importance to many Cree to maintain wildlife hunting as a way to maintain a traditional Cree perspective of the world. The same is true for the Inuit (and other North American Aboriginal groups), who seek to re-instate hunts for formerly depleted species which are now becoming locally available again (Freeman *et al.* 1992).

Subsistence hunting and other land-based economies in general are vulnerable to disruption by industrial developments such as hydroelectric projects, mining, and forestry, with little opportunity for Aboriginal people to control such development or protect the land base that sustains their economies. It is notable in this regard that in 1991-92, the western James Bay Cree strongly rejected the Moose River basin hydroelectric development proposed by Ontario Hydro, with its promises of employment benefits and greater economic integration with the south (Berkes *et al.* 1994).

A common theme in local economic development strategies is to reduce external economic dependence and facilitate growth based on local markets and use of local resources (RCAP 1996). Economic viability based on local resources such as wildlife will not come quickly or easily. An emphasis on small-scale enterprises, compatible with wildlife use and subsistence activities, will be an important component of future local development strategies in the Canadian north. Ecotourism and outfitting (discussed in Chapter 4) are good examples of related market opportunities. The continuing contribution of traditional harvesting activities to community income and employment is an objective for both community sustainability and community economic development. Alternative views of development articulated by Aboriginal people favour a mixed economy, not as a transition to the ideal of a wage economy, but as an arrangement that can persist in a culturally and environmentally sustainable fashion. Thus, viable development strategies for Aboriginal-dominated areas of the Canadian north could involve conserving and utilizing renewable, land- (and sea-) based resources and investing in resource-based industries and local services. Such strategies would protect the traditional economy as a vital and culturally-essential sector, and a cornerstone of the mixed economy.

The planners of the development decade of the 1970s, along with many southern Canadians looking at 'empty' maps of the north, assumed the north was very largely free of human use. The scepticism that met some early studies of Aboriginal land use has given way to a major change in the perception of the Canadian north by the south.

Aboriginal land use and land-based economies persist, and do not seem to be disappearing. The major produce of the land is wildlife, and continued use of wildlife resources remains essential for the exercise and transmission of Aboriginal cultures. Aboriginal people in the Canadian north intend to continue using renewable resources as the basis of an environmentally and culturally sustainable northern economy and society.

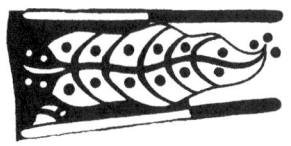

CHAPTER 3:

Commercial harvesting of wild ungulates in Northern Canada

Joe Dragon

Commercial harvesting of wild free-roaming ungulates for meat production has been occurring in remote communities throughout northern Canada for over two decades. Commercial hunting has been defined in many different ways according to the geographical areas where the harvesting has taken place, and the persons conducting the harvests (e.g., Bennett 1982, Caughley and Gunn 1996, Hudson and Cumming 1989, Ramsey and English 1989, Renecker 1991). In this chapter, commercial harvesting implies *organized harvesting of wild ungulates by Aboriginal people for sale in local or export economies.*[18]

During the last century, the domestic economy in northern Canada has evolved from traditional hunter/gatherer activities to a mix of wage earning and harvesting activities (Usher and Weihs 1990). Currently, two Canadian provinces (Quebec and Newfoundland and Labrador) and one territory (the Northwest Territories - NWT) participate in commercial hunting. Since the early 1980s, Inuit and other Aboriginal people have commercially hunted reindeer/caribou (*Rangifer tarandus*) and muskoxen (*Ovibos moschatus*) in the Canadian Arctic. In addition, the Inuit and the Naskapi, Montagnais, and Cree Indians of northern Quebec and Labrador have been commercially harvesting caribou since

---

18. Fish and marine mammals (including polar bears, seals, and in some areas, whales) have been part of the commercial export economy at various times throughout the past 100 years. The Canadian north also supports large populations of bird life, some of which may have the potential to support future commercial harvesting.

the mid-1980s. This chapter briefly describes projects in the provincial norths and provides greater details on the current status of commercial hunting in the NWT.

3.1 Commercial hunting in the provincial north

The caribou populations in northern Quebec and Labrador comprise the George River Herd and the Leaf River Herd, which currently number 800,000 and 260,000 animals, respectively (Lowi 1997).

Quebec—In northern Quebec, the Inuit, Naskapi and Cree Indians have been commercially hunting caribou since a 1994 amendment of their comprehensive claim (the James Bay and Northern Quebec Agreement —JBNQA), which gave them exclusive rights to harvest wild game commercially (Notzke 1994, Drolet *et al.* 1987). Since 1994, three companies have been issued commercial hunting licences in Quebec:

- Nunavik Arctic foods, a subsidiary of Makivik Corporation (quota of 7,200);
- a Naskapi community in Schefferville, Quebec (quota of 3,000);
- the Ipushin Ranch in Inukjuak, Quebec (quota of 5,000) (Lowi 1997).

Nunavik Arctic Foods is licensed to sell meat only in Quebec and has yet to fill its quota. Caribou are hunted by traditional methods which include shooting either in the head or neck so as to reduce wastage. Once killed, animals are eviscerated on the land and then brought back to one of four processing facilities located on the Ungava Bay or Hudson Bay coasts. Animals must be brought to a processing facility within one hour in order to avoid spoilage (Lowi 1997). Once at a processing facility, caribou are skinned, processed and then shipped to distribution markets. The Naskapi community in Schefferville has yet to conduct a hunt, while the Ipushin Ranch combines herding with harvesting and processing at a federally-inspected and regulated facility.

Newfoundland and Labrador—In 1985, the Labrador Inuit Association (LIA) proposed to begin commercially harvesting caribou. In 1986, the Labrador Inuit Development Corporation (LIDC) assumed charge of the operations and was issued a quota of one thousand animals (Notzke 1994). Local Inuit completed pilot projects during their caribou hunting seasons (August to April) to assess the viability of these hunts. Meat inspections, marketing promotions, and a permanent processing facility were developed to enhance the viability of the commercial hunt.

However, the processing facility, located in Nain, Labrador, had structural problems which resulted in its closure.

In 1997, a second commercial hunting licence was issued to a local meat shop (Uncle Sam's Butcher Shop in Goose Bay, Labrador). This experimental commercial hunt, to be located in western Labrador, had an initial quota of 200 animals. The quota could be increased to 500 animals, depending on the success of the operation's start-up and marketing of the product. Uncle Sam's Butcher Shop is an integrated, value-added operation that involves harvesting, cleaning, transportation, processing, and distribution of caribou products (Aylward 1997). Unlike earlier harvesting by the LIDC, which involved only Inuit of the region, both Aboriginal (Innu, Naskapi, and Montagnais Indians) and non-Aboriginal people would be allowed to participate in this experimental commercial hunt (Leboubon 1998).

3.2 Commercial hunting in the Northwest Territories

Commercial hunts of wild free-roaming ungulate herds have been conducted throughout the NWT. Commercial hunting of wild ungulates for meat production varies from region to region and can be divided into three categories:

- market hunting;
- organized community hunts;
- large-scale commercial hunts.

Market Hunting—Market hunting refers to *'the use of animals by individuals for barter and/or cash exchange within the community.'* Market hunting is part of the land-based sector described in Chapter 2 of this paper. Records of this type of wildlife utilization are limited; however, the economic importance of this activity to community residents makes it appropriate for identification. Aboriginal people that are Native to the NWT are eligible to receive a General Hunting License (GHL) which entitles them to harvest as many animals as required for subsistence purposes (Bennett 1982). Depending on which area of the NWT the hunter is in and which species the hunter is obtaining, allowable limits (quotas) may be set by the Government of the Northwest Territories (GNWT). Any quotas are determined within the context of regional co-management regimes, in areas covered by comprehensive claims. [19]

As a way to supplement their income, some GHL holders have started to sell their game to either local meat plants or to other GHL holders. Exchanges between GHL holders can only take place in the NWT; cross-border selling is illegal. Any sales to non-GHL holders require a commercial tag. This hunting practice was initially founded as a traditional act of obtaining game for elders or other people who could not go out on the land. Market hunting has since become a very lucrative side occupation for many hunters in the NWT.

Organized Community Hunts—Local Hunters' and Trappers' Associations (HTAs)[20] throughout the NWT have participated in community hunts of wild ungulates for cash sale within their respective communities. The selling of meat is restricted to the NWT because meat sold across territorial or provincial borders are subject to Federal Meat Inspection Regulations (Gunn *et al.* 1991, see also Section 3.3). Most organized community hunts do not exceed one hundred animals and are based on community quota limits where these are in place. Some hunts are limited because the meat must be sold very quickly in order to avoid spoilage due to limited storage facilities. Organized hunts usually occur over a period of two to five days and hunters are paid for the number of animals taken, and reimbursed for their travel expenses. After the hunt is completed and all animals are butchered, hunters return to their respective communities and sell the meat to community members. HTAs use the money generated to pay hunters for their time

---

19. Commercial hunting quotas are part of the total allowable harvest (TAH) for each species recommended by the wildlife co-management boards established under comprehensive claim settlements. These co-management boards are required to allocate the TAH firstly to meet the beneficiaries' (claimant group members) basic needs level. If and when these basic needs are met, the boards may allocate part of the TAH to non-beneficiaries and commercial use. Commercial tags are distributed to local hunters' and trappers' organizations, who then distribute the tags to members or other hunters.

20. Hunters' and Trapper' Associations (HTAs) exist in all communities in the NWT. Under the terms of comprehensive claim settlements, HTAs may have legislated responsibilities for some aspects of wildlife management. HTAs may also be known by different names under different claim settlements. In the Inuvialuit Settlement Region (ISR) in the western Arctic, for example, local hunters' and trappers' organizations are known as Hunters and Trappers Committees (HTCs).

Commercial harvesting of wild ungulates in northern Canada

and expenses, and/or to fund other local HTA projects. Organized community hunts are seen as a cultural experience and allow local Aboriginal people to participate in a hunt that follows the traditional practice of securing game for those people unable to hunt for themselves.

Large Scale Commercial Hunts—Large-scale commercial hunting of wild ungulates serves external markets (outside the community and/or outside the territory) while providing local employment and cash income. Special programmes of commercial wildlife utilization have been implemented for Aboriginal people of northern Canada (Hudson 1996).

Fig. 3. *Muskoxen. Photo by C. Hickey (August 1978).*

The GNWT has subsidized hunts of caribou and muskoxen in order to generate economic development and/or remove surplus animals to maintain habitat carrying capacity (Gunn *et al.* 1991, Ouellet *et al.* 1993). Caribou have been commercially harvested in the eastern arctic (Southampton Island/Coats Island), central arctic (Victoria Island/Cambridge Bay) and western arctic regions of the NWT. Gunn *et al.* (1991) noted that muskoxen have been harvested primarily from the western arctic since 1981 (Banks Island region) but over the past eight years, harvests in the central arctic (Victoria Island/Cambridge Bay) have gradually increased.

Large-scale commercial hunts are usually organized by HTAs and government. Markets for the meat may be local, national, and/or international. These hunts typically employ 8 to 15 local people and last two to three weeks (Gunn *et al.* 1991, Beaudoin 1990). Depending on the species harvested and allowable quotas, harvests can number as few as 80 animals or as many as 4,000. Portable camps and *abattoirs* are set up to process the animals on the land. The following excerpt from Gunn *et al.* (1991) describes a typical commercial muskox operation on Banks Island, NWT during the early 1980s:

> "The muskoxen herds are rounded up by two to six hunters on snowmobiles and driven to a portable corral with burlap walls. The hunters allow the muskoxen to move up at a walk and remain a distance of several kilometres from the herd to avoid undue excitement of the animals. Some younger animals and bulls lag behind but are not pursued. The animals are rested in the corral for at least three to four hours before being shot and butchered. A shooter takes the animals at a mean kill rate of one animal every eight minutes. The animals are shot in the head in the corral, bled and then dragged by snowmobile about 100 metres to a large tent which serves as a portable abattoir. The animals are decapitated, winched onto a rack, skinned and moved to a hanging rail for evisceration, splitting and trimming (removal of shanks and neck). The carcass is moved outside where it rapidly freezes in the sub-zero ambient temperatures. Finally, the carcass is quartered, the quarters weighed and wrapped in cheesecloth and waxed paper, and packed in plastic lined freezer storage bins on pallets."

In recent years, others forms of harvesting muskoxen have proven to be very successful. For example, 'pulse hunts' in the Cambridge Bay/Victoria Island region presently harvest between fifty and two hundred animals in either the fall or spring seasons. This method involves a small party of hunters that travels to small groups of muskoxen and then harvests the animals on the land. Once the animals are eviscerated, they are brought back to a small portable *abattoir* where they are skinned, split in half, trimmed, wrapped in cheesecloth and delivered to a local meat plant for final processing. Meat is processed into specialty cuts as well as jerky. In addition, hides are sold either raw or scraped and skulls are sold to local craftsmen for carving purposes.

Unfortunately, formal analysis of commercial hunting in the NWT is very limited, with the exception of a paper by Gunn *et al.* (1991) on muskoxen harvesting. Jingfors (1986) noted that even though information on Native wildlife harvests in Canada has been collected for over 40 years, " ...the records are only of limited value due to incomplete, or sporadic, coverage in space and time, lack of systematic sampling techniques and inconsistent, or unknown, reporting dates." The basis and limitations of these data have been discussed by numerous authors including Kelsall (1968), Berger (1977), Smith and Taylor (1977) and Usher *et al.* (1985). The problem of insufficient and undocumented data has plagued commercial hunting projects throughout the Canadian north. Because of a lack of available data, the remaining sections of this paper focus mainly on large-scale commercial hunts. These sections discuss the rationale for government and private industry involvement, aspects of development of the industry, and the future of large-scale commercial hunting in the NWT.

3.3 Government and private industry involvement

In the NWT, development of commercial hunting has been guided by the GNWT in collaboration with the private sector, Aboriginal organizations, and local communities. Commercially hunted wild meat must meet Federal Government standards if it is to be sold outside the NWT. Meat that stays within NWT borders does not have to be inspected for resale but has to meet GNWT guidelines which emulate Federal standards.

The rationale for the introduction of commercial hunting into small, remote northern communities is described by the GNWT (Department of Renewable Resources 1994):

- to promote economic self-reliance at the local level;
- to increase employment opportunities for the resident labour force through education, training, and job creation;
- to maximize opportunities for local retention and investment of profits;
- to influence the pace of development to promote long-term benefits from the use of wildlife resources.

Historical reasoning for the commercial use of free-roaming wildlife was to enable economic development by gainfully employing Aboriginal people in an occupation that was similar to their traditional way of living (see Gunn *et al.* 1991, Scotter and Telfer 1975, Stern *et al.* 1980, Usher 1976, Usher and Weihs 1990). Hunting and acquiring of wildlife plays an integral role in the lives of many northern residents (Freeman 1984, 1997; Wein *et al.* 1996). Renewable resources currently form the subsistence and economic base for both Aboriginal and non-Aboriginal Northerners (Renecker *et al.* 1989), and dependence on wildlife determines the fate of many remote northern communities. Notzke

(1994) describes the current economic situation of northern residents as a result of the combination of the decline of the fur trade, the collapse of the sealing industry and the movement of northern residents to a wage economy (also see Klein 1989). Commercial hunting can contribute to the alternative vision of northern economic development as a mix of subsistence activities and wage employment (see Chapter 2). Commercial hunting has the potential to make a contribution to future northern development that is culturally, economically, and environmentally sustainable.

Commercial harvesting in the NWT is currently monitored by two territorial government departments and one Canadian (Federal) Government department. The territorial departments consist of the Department of Resources, Wildlife and Economic Development (RWED) and the Department of Health and Social Services. RWED has the mandate and legal authority to make regulations pertaining to the use and sale of wildlife and its products. RWED has implemented various regulations for harvesting, processing, sale, and serving of game and game products, as well as environmental requirements for commercial hunting operations (Colford 1998). The Department of Health and Social Services has regulations pertaining to the harvesting of wildlife under the *Public Health Act*. This Act governs sanitary conditions for preparing and serving food. This department has the authority to make regulations and recently-implemented domestic meat inspection regulations that apply to fixed *abattoirs*.

Federal departments involved in commercial hunting include Agriculture and Agrifood Canada. Agrifood Canada oversees the actions of the Canadian Food Inspection Agency (CFIA). Agriculture and Agrifood Canada is involved in ensuring food safety when agricultural products are produced for inter-provincial and international trade. Meat inspection in Canada is a two-tiered system (Gunn *et al.* 1991). Red meat transported across territorial, provincial, or international borders must be federally inspected by approved federal meat inspectors and pass meat standards issued by Agriculture and Agrifood Canada.

Commercial meat production in the NWT involves many participants in both the private and government sectors. Dominant players are the community HTAs and private sector exporters of game meat and marketers of game meat. Local HTAs are now initiating commercial hunts as well as setting up small-scale meat processing facilities which are mainly used for domestic sales. Small-scale meat processing facilities are presently in place in the central and eastern Arctic, as well as in the southern NWT.

Exporters of game meat have included the Umayot Corporation (Banks Island, NWT—discontinued 1994), Tunneq Harvests (Coral

Harbour, NWT) and the Dogrib Game Corporation (Fort Rae, NWT). These operations have primarily focussed on caribou and muskoxen sales. There is currently only one marketer of game meat for products originating in the NWT and that is Grandview Farms based in Ontario. The market for Grandview Farms is export sales where these meats are considered 'exotic' foods.

The NWT Development Corporation (DevCorp) is a government agency responsible for marketing of meat within and outside the NWT. Canadian Arctic Foods, a corporate arm of DevCorp, is specifically mandated to market northern food products. The SCONE Report (NWT Legislative Assembly 1989), was the driving force behind the creation of DevCorp and formed the basis for the current direction of the commercial meat industry in the NWT (Colford 1998).

The laws governing commercial harvesting in the NWT were developed in the 1970s and are currently being updated to more closely reflect today's commercial activities (Colford 1998). Over the past few years, considerable progress has been made to develop territorial guidelines for meat harvesting. Government enforces these guidelines by including them in the issuance of a wildlife licence to the organization completing the hunt. Currently, there is no territorial legislation or delivery system for implementing a meat inspection system; legislation is expected to be in place in the next few years as the commercial use of wildlife increases.

3.4 Obstacles to development of a commercial hunting industry in the NWT

Commercial meat harvesting in the NWT has developed in modest steps since the 1980s. The main objective of government, along with Aboriginal organizations and local communities, was to develop projects that would increase employment opportunities and utilize renewable resources in small remote communities throughout the north. Harvesting of wildlife for commercial use was seen as a productive occupation for Northerners because it would allow for income earning activity and would also utilize traditional skills and knowledge (Gunn *et al.* 1991, Scotter and Telfer 1975). Being able to use their own skills and knowledge would not only promote cultural and family values but would also enhance self-esteem through creation of meaningful employment in remote northern communities (Notzke 1994).

There have been and continue to be two main obstacles to development of the commercial hunting industry in the NWT. These obstacles relate to sustainability of the wildlife populations and marketing of commercially harvested meat.

Sustainability of Northern Wildlife Populations—One of the main concerns about commercial harvesting among Aboriginal people is the ability to sustainably harvest resources without jeopardizing the future of wildlife populations. The erratic nature of northern ungulate populations is well documented (e.g., Caughley 1977, Caughley and Gunn 1996, Ouellet et al. 1993). This concern was addressed by government officials and community residents through the setting of low production goals (i.e., small harvests) while incurring large expenses in capital infrastructure. Infrastructure costs were absorbed through government subsidies that provided capital expenditures while commercial meat harvesting was in its infancy. With exhaustive research into processing techniques, the ability to harvest productively has increased over the years. The reasoning of the GNWT was that if the capital equipment was already in place, the financial burden would be less for communities participating in these operations in future years. In order to ensure wildlife population objectives, local organizations must adhere to quota limitations.

Overall production of wild meat from large-scale commercial hunting in the NWT has increased about 20-fold between the early 1980s and 1997 (J. Dragon, unpublished data). Despite this increased harvest, large-scale commercial hunting is still at a low level, and is believed to have had negligible impact on the large ungulate populations of the NWT.

The increase of harvesting numbers (and meat production) in the NWT can be attributed to a number of factors. Past commercial hunting ventures have had little success largely because of obstacles imposed by stringent meat inspection requirements (Hudson and Cumming 1989) and lack of developed markets (Klein 1989). Some operations have only been able to process a limited number of animals due to logistical constraints, weather conditions, processing capacity and funding restraints. Other limitations to commercial hunting of muskoxen have included low population numbers, their sensitivity to climatic fluctuations and socio-economic and marketing factors (Gunn et al. 1991). However, in one case (Southampton Island, NWT), a commercial harvest of caribou was established based on numbers that would effectively manage population levels. It was felt that without population manipulation or cropping, as discussed in Renecker (1991), this herd would inevitably over-graze its habitat and probably 'crash' due to overpopulation (see Caughley and Gunn 1993,1996; Leader-Williams 1988).

Commercial harvesting of wild ungulates in northern Canada

Present population estimates for muskoxen in the NWT are about 139,000, with 19,000 on the NWT mainland and another 120,000 on the Arctic islands (Fournier and Gunn 1997). Population estimates for each of the NWT's caribou herds are currently being developed. There are well over one million caribou on the mainland NWT, while the Southampton Island caribou population is estimated at about 29,000 (Gunn 1998). Current populations of both caribou and muskoxen are at high levels and are experiencing very high productivity. At the same time, the commercial hunting quotas for the entire NWT are 8,300 and 8,000 animals, respectively. Caribou quotas are being used at fifty per cent of the total allowable limit, whereas muskoxen quotas are being used at between fifteen and twenty percent (Colford 1998).

Marketing—Marketing has been one of the main obstacles to development of successful commercial harvesting in the NWT. Within territorial borders, wild meat has had difficulty competing with southern meat products (e.g., beef, pork, and poultry) as store-bought food. Most NWT residents have relatively easy access to wild meat obtained through subsistence hunting (see Chapter 2) and view store-bought wild meat not as a regular fare but rather as a special occasion item (Colford 1998). Past problems with introduction of wild meat to territorial (and other) markets are numerous and include:

- inadequate distribution network,
- limited processing capability,
- lack of information,
- an imperfect track record with regard to product quality and price,
- inconsistency of supply,
- lack of an effective inspection system, leaving a less than perfect impression among discerning consumers (Colford 1998).

Wild meat as a store-bought food is a relatively new product for NWT consumers. In order for this product to gain acceptance domestically (as well as internationally), it must be competitively priced, highly visible, and widely available to the consumer (Krieg 1989).

3.5 Future prospects for commercial harvesting in northern Canada

Attitudes toward the sustainable use of wildlife resources have been scarred by past disasters with wildlife populations (Noss 1995). In the past, it was realized that exploiters of a common pool resource stocks had little incentive for conservation of that resource (Clark 1991). Some examples of this phenomenon can be seen in the collapse of the Atlantic cod fishery (Mackenzie 1995), the downfall of the bowhead whale fishery in the western Arctic (Conrad 1989), and the exploitation and demise of the anchoveta fishery in Peru during the 1970s (Idyll 1973), to name a few. These failures to sustainably use resources can be attributed to several factors including overcapitalization, increased technological advances in harvesting techniques, and political pressure to continue harvesting (Clark 1991, Caughley and Gunn 1996). This phenomenon has been commonly referred to as 'the tragedy of the commons' (Hardin 1968), with the inevitable result being degradation of the resource and ultimate impoverishment of all resource users (Clark 1991). Recently however, a growing literature has pointed to conditions under which common property resources have been successfully managed on a sustainable basis (e.g., Berkes *et al.* 1989, Ostrom 1990, National Research Council 1986, McCay and Acheson 1987).

The future of commercial wildlife production in the NWT is a potentially prosperous one. Recent success in the commercial hunting industry can be attributed to the active partnerships developed between different levels of government, different departments of government, and commercial harvesters. Current industry priorities include developing technology and processing techniques to utilize unfilled quotas and to ensure a quality product for the northern market (Colford 1998). Residents of northern communities are poised for significant potential economic benefits from commercial harvesting. They have a wide range of experience in these types of ventures and are benefiting from government policies of community empowerment with regard to wildlife resources. This 'ownership' concept is envisioned as one of the keys for success in ventures of this nature (Notzke 1994).

A key factor in the future success of commercial harvesting in northern Canada is the scale of harvesting. This must be appropriate both for the wildlife populations and the Aboriginal communities of the north. Subsistence hunting will continue to be the first priority for harvesting of wildlife in the Canadian north, and commercial quotas must be determined in this context. Commercial quotas must also take into account the erratic nature of many northern wildlife populations. At some point, limits may need to be placed on the amount of investment in infrastructure for commercial harvesting in the Canadian north, in order to reduce potential political pressure to continue harvesting in the face of declining wildlife populations. If governments and community residents can ensure development of this industry at an appropriate scale, the outlook for commercial hunting is very positive for the Aboriginal people of Canada's Northwest Territories.

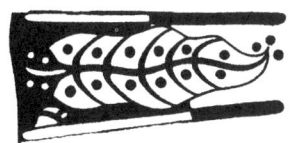

CHAPTER 4:

Aboriginal community involvement in wildlife tourism: The Canadian experience

Claudia Notzke

Community involvement in wildlife management by means of co-management regimes has experienced its greatest proliferation and longest track record in northern Canada, within the framework of the comprehensive claim settlement process. This paper therefore focusses on the north, particularly the Northwest Territories (NWT). The NWT and the Yukon Territory are covered by a mosaic of comprehensive claims, the settlement of which has reached varying stages of negotiation and implementation. Correspondingly, this huge area is also covered by co-management regimes for wildlife and other renewable resources, which vary widely in origin, history, maturity, and focus.

Significantly for the topic at hand, in 1983 the Government of the NWT (GNWT) launched its *Community-Based Tourism Strategy* (GNWT 1983). While wildlife co-management regimes and wildlife-based tourism (mostly hunting, fishing, and burgeoning ecotourism) are also encountered in the James Bay region of northern Quebec, and are aspired to by other Canadian Aboriginal groups (Notzke 1994), examples from the NWT offer the most food for thought and the most interesting lessons and prospects.

4.1 Context for community-based wildlife tourism

Examination of the nature of community-based tourism with a focus on wildlife requires at least superficial familiarity with the context of wildlife use and tourism, in terms of the socio-economic, management, and tourism environment.

Northern Communities and Economies—Northern Canadian communities are small, seldom numbering more than several hundred inhabitants. Their populations are predominantly Aboriginal as well as young and fast-growing. By national standards they possess very modest physical infrastructures. They are geographically remote from non-Aboriginal population centres and are located in relatively pristine natural environments. These communities feature mixed economies in which incomes are derived from a mix of domestic production, wage labour, transfers, and enterprise. Due to the high cost of living in the Canadian north, life would be problematic in many small communities without income from domestic production, i.e., hunting, fishing, trapping, and gathering.

Figure 4. *Fish camp at Stewart River, NWT. Photo by M. Ivanitz (CCI archives).*

Although domestic production makes a very significant contribution to the local economies of northern communities, little of this contribution is in the form of cash. Because all needs cannot be

Aboriginal community involvement in wildlife tourism

satisfied through domestic production alone, it would be equally difficult to continue life in northern communities without cash. Cash incomes are earned through sale of labour, commodities, and enterprise. Of these activities, wage labour is most important, but rarely are there enough jobs for all people who want employment, and employment opportunities usually grow more slowly than the labour force. Domestic production cannot provide for all needed goods and services, nor can employment, commodities, and enterprise yield all needed cash. Northern communities are therefore sustained partially by transfers from the outside. In mixed economies, no one sector takes precedence over any other; the sectors are mutually supportive to the extent that should one sector fail, the entire economy would be in jeopardy (Elias 1995).

Fig. 5. *Caribou hunting in Yukon. Photo by M. Ivantiz (CCI archives).*

Within this framework, domestic production continues to be viewed as the most reliable sector of the mixed northern economy, as well as the main source of cultural satisfaction and social prestige (see Chapter 2). Ideas of how life should be lived are fundamentally tied to being on the land. Rather than detracting from this valuation, cash income adds to it. Cash is used not only to supply households with consumer goods and services, but also to underwrite the costs of domestic production. When households have cash available, they spend it on technology and transportation to reach distant harvesting sites more quickly, to enable them to produce more costly prestige resources (e.g., beluga, caribou), and to enhance their redistributive status within the community.

The importance of cash in northern economies is likely to increase in the future. For this reason, most households, whether or not they are dedicated domestic producers, will welcome any initiative that increases access to cash. But given what was said above, it is hardly surprising that there is much individual determination and collective political will to safeguard domestic resources from trespass and competition from cash-producing activities, be they resource-based or not. This objective is achieved by the process of co-management (discussed in Chapter 1; see also Notzke 1993, 1995a), which creates an operational environment with this priority in mind. Co-management regimes strive to provide a regulatory environment that makes allowance for both traditional and innovative modes of resource utilization. These are complex regimes for any industry, including tourism, to operate in, as they endeavour to be compatible with Aboriginal values and with the nature of socio-economic change and continuity as perceived by Aboriginal societies.

The Northwest Territories Tourism Industry—The NWT is an enormous geographic area representing one-third of Canada.[21] The nature of destination attractions and the level of tourism product development throughout this vast region are not uniform.[22] Large parts of Nunavut (the eastern and central Arctic) are at a developmental stage in terms of tourism product development and delivery, while the Yellowknife/Great Slave and south Mackenzie areas of the southwestern NWT have a critical mass of both attractions and tourist industry infrastructure. The western Arctic is the only part of Canada's Arctic that is accessible by road, namely the famous Dempster Highway. Here the town of Inuvik constitutes 'the end of the Dempster' and serves as

---

21. The total area of the Northwest Territories is 3,376,698 km^2 or 1,304,903 mi^2. The NWT represents one-third of the total area of Canada and is approximately the same size as India. In 1996, the total (human) population of the NWT was 64,402. On April 1, 1999, the NWT was divided into two territories. The eastern territory "Nunavut" was one of the results of the Nunavut comprehensive claim.

22. Tourist attractions include spectacular scenery, wildlife viewing, unspoiled wilderness, and opportunities to experience Aboriginal culture. The availability and accessibility of tourist attractions varies widely from region to region.

Aboriginal community involvement in wildlife tourism

the major transportation hub and staging point for the western Arctic region. While the Dempster holds tremendous market potential, significant product development will be necessary before the western Arctic can more effectively capture this potential and hold visitors long enough to enhance the economic impact of Dempster Highway travellers (Derek Murray Consulting Associates *et al.* 1994).

According to the 1994 NWT Exit Survey, over 6,300 people visited Inuvik during the 1994 summer tourist season, mostly via the Dempster Highway. This constitutes approximately 19 percent of all visitors to the NWT, compared to almost 24,000 visitors or 70 percent to the south Mackenzie and over 3,500 travellers or 11 percent to the eastern Arctic (GNWT 1995). In all three survey areas, domestic Canadian travellers accounted for by far the largest proportion of visitors, representing 76 percent and 88 percent in the south Mackenzie and eastern Arctic, respectively. However, in the Dempster Highway/Inuvik area, the proportion of Canadians was much lower, at 54 percent, with 25 percent originating from the United States, and 21 percent from outside North America (GNWT 1995). The larger American proportion is attributed to the proximity of Alaska. The 1992 Western Arctic Visitor Survey (Bufo Inc. 1992a, b) tells us something about these travellers' primary interests: as has been recorded in most of North America, wildlife viewing ranked first with 99 percent of visitors choosing it as one of their main interests. 'Native culture' followed as a close second with 96 percent (Bufo Inc. 1992b). It is therefore reasonable to conclude that a combination of the two interests, namely wildlife-related activities paired with an 'Aboriginal tourism experience' would hold particular appeal for most northern travellers.

Tourism and Protected Areas—Community involvement with tourism in protected areas varied widely throughout the NWT. Some parks are very remote from communities, and in these cases there may be relatively little community involvement. Other parks are located very close to communities and local residents may be intimately involved with park management and tourism activities. In other cases, parks have been established for many years, but only recently have communities become involved in tourism activities within these parks.

Historically, all hunting was prohibited within Canadian National Parks, and sport hunting is still prohibited within park boundaries. There are cases, in both southern and northern Canada, where the establishment of protected areas resulted in the exclusion of Aboriginal people (see Notzke 1994). Traditional hunting, fishing and trapping activities began to be recognized within National Parks starting in the 1920s. Subsistence harvesting activities are now permitted within most

National Parks in the NWT, and numerous parks have been created as a result of comprehensive claim settlements. Depending on the provisions of the claim settlement under which a park was created, Aboriginal people may have preferential rights to tourism-related opportunities within some parks. Many National Parks created under comprehensive claim settlements are relatively recent, and the future is likely to see increased involvement of Aboriginal communities in tourism activities in northern National Parks.

4.2 Sport hunting

There are two major categories of wildlife-based tourism in the NWT: sport hunting and non-consumptive activities. Sport hunting is the variety of tourism which has the longest tradition in the north. Sport hunters are by far the highest per capita spenders of all visitors, and thus, even in small numbers, may have a considerable impact on community economies. For the NWT as a whole, approximately 9,708 visitors engaged in hunting or fishing, compared to 12,555 people auto touring and 8,286 drawn to the north by outdoor adventure (Derek Murray Consulting Associates *et al.* 1994). At present, fishing and hunting is the NWT's single largest tourism product in terms of annual revenue at $14.1 million (compared to $10.7 million for auto touring and $12.8 million for outdoor adventure). Of the estimated 9,708 fishing/hunting visitors, 8,902 are associated with fishing, and 806 with hunting. If the revenue figures were broken down further, they would more than likely reveal a disproportionately large contribution by hunting clients.

Aboriginal people in the NWT are well positioned to take advantage of this industry. Non-resident hunters are required to enlist the services of a licensed outfitter to hunt big game. Outfitters provide licensed guides for the hunters they serve. Hunts for polar bear, barren-ground grizzly bear, and muskox can be conducted only by community wildlife management organizations (Hunters' and Trappers' Associations or Hunters' and Trappers' Committees) acting as outfitters. Hunts for polar bear must be done in the traditional way, using dog teams.[23]

---

23. Outfitting requirements vary depending on species, region, and the specific harvesting rights outlined in comprehensive claim settlements. Non-Aboriginal outfitters, including some from southern Canada, guided sport hunters in the Mackenzie Mountains along the NWT-Yukon border for many years. In other regions, Aboriginal people have exclusive outfitting rights derived from comprehensive claim settlements. Under these settlements, the "exclusive" harvesting rights

Aboriginal community involvement in wildlife tourism

In the western Arctic, there is sport hunting for polar bear, muskox, tundra grizzly bear, and caribou. Sport hunting is not a 'growth industry,' and there are various trends in the market, depending on species. Polar bear hunts are considered the 'top hunt' in the north, and probably have the best chance of 'holding their own' or even increasing the number of bookings, particularly in view of recent changes to the *Marine Mammal Protection Act* in the United States (Stephen *et al.* 1993). This changed legislation makes it easier to import polar bear trophies into the United States. The northern market potential must also be viewed against the background of an overall worldwide decline in opportunities for sport hunting, which puts the continued access to high quality resources in the NWT in a particularly favourable light. On the other hand, the emerging attitude of the 1990s is one of resource conservation, which may negatively impact consumptive outdoor activities. The most important markets for sport hunting are the United States and Europe, particularly Germany, Spain, and Italy. Annually, approximately 60 polar bear hunts are sold and fulfilled by outfitters in the NWT, and around 100 muskox hunts (Stephen *et al.* 1993).

Within the Inuvialuit Settlement Region (the area covered by the comprehensive claim settlement of the Inuit of the western Arctic), the most active sport hunting communities are Sachs Harbour (with the longest sport hunting tradition), Holman, and to a lesser degree, Paulatuk and Tuktoyaktuk. One of the major issues facing the Aboriginal people involved in this industry is reconciliation of the communal character of customary renewable resource use with the private enterprise and competitive aspect of sport hunting (Interview with Bruce Hanbidge—Inuvik, 12 July 1995). The Renewable Resources Committees established by the *Inuvialuit Final Agreement* (IFA) play an important part in this industry by determining quotas of 'limited species' such as polar bear, grizzly, and muskox. The communal aspect of the hunt is maintained by the community Hunters' and Trappers' Committees (HTCs), which function as the licensed outfitters. Through the co-management process, quotas for big game species are recommended by co-management boards and then allocated by government to the community HTCs. For financial management reasons, most HTCs have incorporated their sport hunt business: for example, Banks Island Big Game Hunts (Sachs Harbour HTC), Beaufort

---

of Aboriginal people generally include the rights of assignment to other (sport) hunters, as well as the rights to guiding and outfitting. Outfitting requirements and restrictions on methods of hunting are outlined in the territorial *Wildlife Acts*.

Outfitting and Guiding Services (Tuktoyaktuk HTC), and Holman Sports Hunts (Ulukhaktomiut HTC). The HTCs sub-allocate tags to individual hunters/guides and outfitters. These community corporations do some of their own bookings but also use booking agents in eastern Canada and the United States.

Prior to 1990, sport hunts in the western Arctic were booked through Guided Arctic Expeditions (GAE), a corporation owned by the Inuvialuit Game Council (IGC), who also determined GAE's course of action by policy directives. The philosophy of GAE was to commercialize wildlife to the maximum degree permissible by conservation limits. GAE had one full-time employee, a manager based in Inuvik, who was responsible for marketing and liaison, and also made arrangements for clients as they arrived in Inuvik. Contact with the communities was maintained through the IGC and the HTCs, who chose the guides or outfitters. When GAE ran into cash flow problems, it was replaced by a more decentralized system, dominated by the HTCs, that is in operation today (Interview with Norman Snow—Inuvik, 24 July 1995).

The operation of this community-based sport hunting system varies slightly from community to community. Like GAE, the communities' sport hunting corporations occasionally assist guides and outfitters with technology and equipment. The system is essentially self-regulating, since problems such as insufficient service to a client, lack of expertise, abuse of a dog team or waste of any kind, may easily result in a community (rather than an individual) being blacklisted. Sport hunters are well connected through local or regional clubs and associations; a satisfied customer can therefore be an outfitter's best marketing agent. Naturally, this system can also work against an outfitter. A system of 'tribal justice' is meted out against abusers of the system; punishment may go as far as barring an individual from guiding for life. Obviously, the system is also open to abuse 'from the top,' due to the influence of politics. The allocation of tags and clients to individual guides or outfitters may be highly discretionary. As unfortunately happens in many Aboriginal communities unaccustomed to social and economic stratification, success may breed envy, which in turn may result in political repercussions (see Notzke 1995b for more details).

Even though their numbers are relatively small, sport hunters are making a substantial contribution to community economies, and there is potential for even greater contributions. A polar bear hunt costs approximately $23,000 (Cdn.), a tundra grizzly bear $5,200, a muskox $3,800, and two caribou $3,000. The money goes directly to the community corporations, who are responsible for determining and distributing payment to outfitters and guides. Considering the more active communities, there are 15 licensed guides in Tukotyaktuk for polar bear, muskox, grizzly bear, and caribou (interview with Lloyd Gruben—Tuktoyaktuk, 19 July 1995), and 23 in Sachs Harbour (Stephen *et al.* 1993). In 1995, the Tuktoyaktuk quota for polar bears was 26, of which a maximum of 50 percent could be taken by sports hunters. Furthermore, 12 grizzly bear tags were set aside for sport hunters along with 254 muskoxen and 175 commercial caribou tags. In Sachs Harbour in 1993, the HTC allocated 16 polar bear tags and 500 muskox tags for sport hunting; 14 muskox hunters and one polar bear hunter were actually booked. During the winter of 1994-1995, seven of nine sport hunters in Holman got their polar bears and there were numerous muskox sport hunts (ICS 1995a). According to Lloyd Gruben, GNWT Renewable Resource Officer for Tuktoyaktuk, there is much interest in big game guiding on the part of younger people (ICS 1995a).

Figure 6. *Polar Bear. Photo by J. Ramsay (CCI Archives).*

The above example from the western Arctic illustrates that big game sport hunting is the variety of tourism with the deepest roots and longest history in northern Canadian communities. Hunters are the largest per capita spenders in the tourism industry; they demand less of a tourism infrastructure than many other tourists, and they do not, on ideological grounds, object to a northern land-based harvesting way of life. Promotion and marketing of sport hunts is by word of mouth through satisfied clients, and via established linkages with local or regional clubs and associations. All these factors make sport hunters very attractive clients for Aboriginal communities. On the other hand, it must be acknowledged that sport hunting in the NWT is, at best, a stable industry, whereas growth potential lies with ecotourism and adventure tourism, in short with non-consumptive outdoor activities. What is the relationship between these two important subsectors of the tourism industry? Not surprisingly, there are differing opinions on this subject.

Peter Lamb of Parks Canada (interview—Inuvik, 13 July 1995) feels that the long history of, and extensive participation in big game outfitting on the part of many communities is one reason why ecotourism will be able to evolve only over a longer period of time in the north. While both activities are resource-based, they require profoundly different 'people skills' from tourism operators. Aboriginal operators themselves express less ambivalence about combining the two subsectors, as long as common-sense rules are followed such as cleaning up the hunting camp and keeping the operations separate (interviews with Maureen Pokiak—Tuktoyaktuk 18 July 1995 and Randal Pokiak—Tuktoyaktuk, 19 July 1995). Aboriginal people do not necessarily perceive a contrast between the various ways in which the land and its resources sustain them: be it by harvesting, guiding sport hunters, or catering to ecotourists. James Pokiak of Tuktoyaktuk, who pursues all three activities, expresses it best when he says: "There is a time to harvest the animals, and there is a time to just sit back and enjoy them ..." (ICS 1995b).

4.3 Ecotourism and nature tourism

While wildlife viewing ranks first on the 'wish list' of most northern travellers, it would be misleading to compare non-consumptive tourism activities in northern Canada with safari tourism in eastern and southern Africa. Many travellers to the north return with unforgettable memories of spectacular wildlife encounters, but generally speaking, such encounters are neither predictable nor can they be guaranteed. Only the annual caribou migrations at selected locations present images reminiscent of the teeming herds of Africa's plains. More commonly, encounters with animals are an integral part of an overall immersion in the Arctic or subarctic ecosystem, including the way of life of northern peoples.

Tourists can realize such immersion in various ways: by community tours, in Inuit or Dene (Indian) camps out on the land, on independent or guided visits to parks or park reserves, on a variety of naturalist

Aboriginal community involvement in wildlife tourism

and/or cultural tours (organized by both local and southern operators), and by staying in lodges in selected locations.

Community involvement in such activities is direct as well as indirect. One of the most important aspects of tourism development in the north is the fact that co-management regimes provide the operational environment for the industry. These regimes encompass all aspects of environmental management, i.e., in addition to wildlife management in the narrower 'western' sense, there is environmental impact assessment and review, and the establishment and management of protected areas. As a result, northern communities have considerable influence on tourism developments, particularly where wildlife is concerned, and especially where comprehensive claim settlements have been finalized.

Aboriginal communities and individuals are increasingly taking advantage of opportunities to become directly involved in 'land-based' tourism, although a vast potential remains largely untapped. In this context, the advent of 'ecotourism' plays a major role. Ecotourism is the fastest-growing and most dynamic segment of the tourism industry.

The Ecotourism Society in Bennington, Vt., defines ecotourism as:

> *"Responsible travel to natural areas that conserves the environment and sustains the well-being of local people."* (Merlino 1993:4).

In a similar vein, the Adventure Travel Society sees ecotourism as:

> *"Environmentally responsible travel to experience the natural areas and culture of a region while promoting conservation and economically contributing to local communities."* (Adventure Travel Society 1994:2).

Throughout the 1980s, ecotourism evolved from 'nature tourism,' by adding a human element. Travellers began to realize that 'nature' is more than a series of spectacular wild species that exist in isolation. They perceived the environment as an interrelated, ever-changing landscape of which people are a part (MacDonald 1993). The next step was the realization that culturally and ecologically responsible travel can generate profits and promote conservation and management of natural areas for long-term sustainable development.

While disadvantaged in many other economic ventures, Aboriginal people in the Canadian north have a competitive edge in ecotourism, for example:

- They are frequently in control of and knowledgeable about vast remote areas.
- They may be able to capitalize on the widespread 'image' of indigenous people living in harmony with their environment.
- While many visitors may be interested in nature *per se*, the opportunity to see the land through Native eyes, and to experience cultural activities, adds an extra and unique element to the trip.

Within a framework of Aboriginal participation in all aspects of renewable resource management, both inside and outside protected areas in the north, there is increasing awareness of the potential of ecotourism development in this vast region. This goes hand-in-hand with the GNWT strategy of 'community-based tourism' development. Pangnirtung, gateway to Auyuittuq National Park in the eastern Arctic, was to serve as a model or pilot project for community-based tourism development. Tourism's economic benefits to the community by means of outfitting, transportation, and arts and craft sales have been significant. The GNWT's approach to its own policy of community-based tourism development, however, is qualified by the fact that 'community-based' does not imply community control, but merely community involvement. In Pangnirtung, the major accomplishment of the community-based approach has been empowerment of the local community to create its own unique mix of formal and non-formal cash-related activities in the tourism industry, which best meets the needs of local families and the community as a whole (Reimer and Dialla 1992).

Other communities are getting ready for the ecotourism challenge. On southern Baffin Island, the Soper River, locally known as Kuujuaq, has been declared a Canadian Heritage River, and its valley has become part of Katannilik Territorial Park. Young people from adjacent Kimmirut (Lake Harbour) are preparing to understand their ancestral landscape from the perspective of outsiders, in order to be able to supplement their incomes by mediating between their homeland and ecotourists who will come to pay it homage (Moss 1994). The Katannilik project has enjoyed the full support of the people of Lake Harbour as a result of their direct involvement in its development and management. The economic impact is already considerable: air fare and hotel accommodation are major factors in the regional economy, while guiding services, other hosting activities, and arts and craft sales stimulate the local economy.

Ecotourism ventures involving Aboriginal people are not confined to the protected areas network. Bathurst Inlet Lodge in the central

Aboriginal community involvement in wildlife tourism

Arctic was established as a naturalist lodge in 1969 by longtime (non-Aboriginal) northerners, long before the term "ecotourism" was even coined. It became an Inuit partnership in the mid-1980s, when Kingaunmiut Ltd. was formed to take care of the financial interests of the people of Bathurst Inlet, and the Inuit became co-owners of the Lodge. The community participates in all aspects of the operation, from directors on the board to kitchen staff and wildlife guides (Butler 1990). Community members play a particularly vital role in the Lodge's educational programmes (Burt *et al.* 1993). The economic impact on this small community is considerable, since the Lodge sells a high-priced, high-value product.

Further west, the Inuvialuit offer visitors an experience on the land, with visits to hunting and fishing camps, in conjunction with homestay programs. To date, their main product consists of community tours in Tuktoyaktuk. The Inuvialuit Settlement Region (ISR) encompasses three National Parks and one Territorial Park, where the Inuvialuit not only have guaranteed management input but also a guaranteed share of tourism benefits.

4.4 Tourism and the land-based economy

In the western Arctic, most of the measures to regulate and control tourism (and other activities) are designed to protect the natural resource base of the ISR and the integrity of Inuvialuit harvesting activities. It is the Inuvialuit vision that what the land provides will always remain central to Inuvialuit life, modern economic aspirations notwithstanding. For this reason, it is very important to examine the relationship between the Inuvialuit land-based economy and the tourism industry. In this context, the challenge for the Inuvialuit in embracing tourism is twofold:

1. To protect the integrity of their land-based economy and way of life from trespass and interference from the tourism industry;
2. To engage in tourism industry activities in a way that enables tourism to fit into, nurture, and benefit community mixed economies to an optimum degree.

The Inuvialuit have responded to the first challenge in a constructive way by developing *Tourism Guidelines for Beluga-Related Tourism Activities* (IGC 1994). Considering Aboriginal peoples' experience with the animal rights movement, the Inuvialuit have every reason to be extremely wary of granting the public access to their harvesting activities.[24] Whaling is the most important harvesting activity during the summer tourist season, and consequently the activity of greatest concern to local communities. The *Tourism Guidelines* are an integral part of the Beaufort Sea Beluga Management Plan (FJMC 1991) and are designed to prevent physical interference with whaling as well as misrepresentation of the activity. The guidelines provide the community HTCs with authority to strictly control access and other activities in the harvesting zones, camps, and vicinities thereof, and they clearly stipulate that subsistence hunting takes priority over any tourism activities.

The summer of 1995 was the first season the *Guidelines* were in effect. There was only one operator who occasionally took visitors to his family's whaling camp, but his trips were irregular and difficult to schedule. The implementation of the *Beluga Tourism Guidelines* is likely to put harvesters more at ease, since the guidelines specifically address harvesters' concerns and give them an element of control. The number of hunters welcoming tourists into their camps will likely remain small but among the Inuvialuit, there are numerous strong believers in the educational function of tourism. These individuals feel that wherever there is a willing host, tourism can go a long way in changing outsiders' views of harvesting activities. An element of risk remains, though: "How do you control information, once you have given it?" (Interview with Richard Binder—Inuvik, 24 July 1995). But with an increasing measure of control on the part of the harvesters and improving education of tourists, more Aboriginal hosts may be willing to take this leap of faith.

Conversations with Inuvialuit hosts and southern guests leave little doubt that an 'Aboriginal tourism experience' is a very effective teacher about the northern way of life. The future of ecotourism, however, will be determined, at least in part, by how well it can be made to fit into this way of life. This is the second challenge referred to earlier. Some of the people who are making the richest contribution to a visitor's northern experience are enabled to do so by the fact that they are not full-time tourism professionals, but are firmly rooted in a way of life that ties them to the land. The tourism part of their mixed economy provides cash to supply their households with consumer goods, and underwrites the cost of their domestic production.

---

24. There are large risks associated with the exposure of Aboriginal harvesting to outsiders, as previous experience has included public outcries and boycotts. Education programmes to introduce outsiders to Aboriginal culture and society will likely be a critical element in the future development of ecotourism in northern Canada.

Aboriginal community involvement in wildlife tourism

The local operators for Arctic Nature Tours in Tuktoyaktuk, NWT, James and Maureen Pokiak, provide an excellent example of how this can be accomplished. The Pokiaks not only combine a land-based way of life with tourism, they also pursue both ecotourism and guiding and outfitting of sport hunters. The Pokiak's current seasonal cycle is outlined in Table 4.1. With careful scheduling of activities, this family is able to spend almost ten months each year out on the land. The Pokiaks come across as genuinely enjoying what they are doing, and tourists respond to this attitude. They also report considerable interest in land-based tourism on the part of younger people, whenever they are looking for employees.

Table 4.1 Seasonal cycle of community residents combining a land-based way of life with tourism activities.

Date	Activity
September	sport hunt for caribou, fish for subsistence and dog food
late October-December	trapping; Christmas break
January-February	trapping, preparation for polar bear hunt
March-April	sport hunt for polar bear, muskox, and barren ground grizzly bear
May	traditional spring hunt for geese (subsistence only), ice fishing, future attraction of 'spring tourists', with dog team rides and visits to local landforms
June	tourists start arriving
June 20-July 23 (approx.)	River rafting trips in Ivvavik National Park
June-August	whaling, community tours

4.5 The future of wildlife-based tourism in northern Canada

Wildlife-oriented tourism comprises two major categories: consumptive and non-consumptive activities. Canada's northern Aboriginal communities look back on a long tradition of consumptive use of wildlife. Due to factors such as strict regulation, small numbers, limited community contact, high capital outlay on the part of the hunter, and minimum leakage,[25] big-game hunting appears to be relatively conflict-free for Aboriginal communities. However, the reconciliation of communal resource use traditions with the entrepreneurial and competitive aspects of big game sport hunting presents challenges for northern communities. Without further research, it is difficult to assess the magnitude of these challenges, but they appear to be manageable. While no quantitative analysis has been attempted here, it seems that supply currently exceeds demand in this industry.

Sport hunting is not a growth industry in the NWT, but considering northern Canada's market position (and assuming animal population stability), 'top hunts,' such as polar bear, may well continue to provide a substantial income to northern communities. Evidence to date indicates that income from outfitting sport hunters has not overridden community conservation concerns (Notzke 1994).

The situation is much more complex for non-consumptive tourism activities. Northern Canada is faced with fewer problems of 'damage control' and alienation of local communities than East African countries, where indigenous populations have experienced displacement and exclusion as a result of conservation and tourism initiatives. Nevertheless, much remains to be done in terms of educating all stakeholders in the industry—local communities, industry, government, and travellers—about the potential as well as the pitfalls of nature-based tourism.

While successful local initiatives are on the increase, there is a need for more widespread recognition, by community leadership and the public, that tourism (if properly controlled and realistically assessed) can really benefit northern communities. A more sophisticated

---

25. "Leakage" refers to lack of a multiplier effect within the community. Leakage can be minimized through the use of local supplies and services (e.g., employment of local guides, serving bush meat to tourists).

Aboriginal community involvement in wildlife tourism

understanding of how these benefits can occur is slow in coming, even in communities such as Tuktoyaktuk and Pangnirtung.

The problem of leakage of tourism dollars can be addressed by increasing the number of local operators and improving linkages between the tourism industry and local supplies and services. In their study of Pond Inlet, Grekin and Milne (1996) present interesting observations regarding missed economic opportunities due to a lack of communication and coordination between various community actors, in areas such as arts and crafts production and accommodation and meals. In the western Arctic, Inuvik's two major tour companies are majority Aboriginal-owned. In other areas, there is still a strong reliance on partnerships between local providers of a tourism product and southern tour operators, with mixed results for northern communities.

Some of the most important challenges facing northern Native peoples relate to the Aboriginal land-based way of life, to questions of how this way of life can be protected from tourism, and how tourism can be shaped to fit into this way of life. The Inuvialuit in the western Arctic have addressed these problems in a proactive manner by means of their *Tourism Guidelines for Beluga-Related Tourism Activities* and their unequivocal statement of priorities. This has not happened everywhere. Grekin and Milne (1996) report on the delicate relationship between tourism and Inuit hunting activities in Pond Inlet, NWT, and the adoption of an 'unwritten' policy to conceal hunting from tourists. On the other hand, ecotourism offers an unmatched opportunity for northern Aboriginal people to educate southerners about the nature of a land-based way of life and everything it entails. This opportunity has been recognized by both northern hosts and southern guests, and there is much indication that Aboriginal people are meeting with a receptive audience (Notzke 1995b). An element of risk, however, remains.

Northern Aboriginal communities and ecotourism are both in a state of rapid evolution, and their interface is a complicated one. Furthermore, both are operating in a highly fragile and unpredictable ecosystem. The future of tourism in this region, as visitors now encounter it, is inexorably bound to the evolution of northern local economies. In this evolution, tourism has the potential for acting as an agent of change as well as an agent of preservation. The 'authenticity' and 'real life character' of the current tourism experience represents an asset as well as a significant management challenge. More tourists and more professionalism will make the industry easier to manage, but what will be lost in the process?

Ecotourism has many faces and can be very flexible. It does not in all cases necessitate major capital outlay on the part of the hosting community, such as a luxury lodge. Tourists can be attracted to homestay programmes and outpost camps, and they can become 'participant observers' of land-based activities. It is necessary, however, for northern hosts to become better educated about their guests' backgrounds and expectations, just as it is important for southern visitors to become better informed about certain realities of northern life. Worldwide trends in ecotourism also clearly indicate the necessity of revisiting ecotourism guide training (Jenks 1997).

The ecotourism industry is becoming increasingly competitive. Both supply and demand are constantly rising, and the ecotraveller is becoming increasingly sophisticated and better educated. Visiting remote areas of the planet remains a cachet that captures the consumer. Increasingly, ecotravel businesses compel themselves to sell a more in-depth exploration of ecosystems and to have greater contact with local communities. There is also an increasing probability of 'return volume,' as travellers return to previously visited sites (Epler-Wood 1997). All this holds much potential for northern Aboriginal communities, while at the same time challenging them to become better educated about the industry, in order to fully capitalize on their potential. This could be particularly worthwhile in cases where new protected areas have been established relatively close to Aboriginal communities, such as Katannilik Territorial Park near Kimmirut (Lake Harbour) and Tuktut Nogait National Park near Paulatuk.

Grekin and Milne (1996) call our attention to the fact that the literature in general has downplayed the role that local people can play in influencing the path of tourism development. This is particularly true for Canada's northern communities. While the results of the comprehensive claims process are by no means satisfactory to all parties, the co-management regimes resulting from this process have empowered Aboriginal communities to take an active role in local tourism development. Canada's northern communities are in a better position than local communities in many other parts of the world to ensure that wildlife tourism or ecotourism remains sustainable and does not undermine their natural and socio-cultural resource base.

CHAPTER 5:

The status of game ranching among Canada's Aboriginal people

Tanja Schramm and Robert J. Hudson

Over the last two decades, game ranching has become a rapidly increasing sector in Canadian agriculture. Currently, farming of various species of deer alone is experiencing a yearly growth rate of about 20 percent and the national herd reached 98,000 in 1997 (Thorleifson 1998). In this paper, *game ranching* refers to "the extensive production of wild ungulates on fenced or open range lands." *Game farming* is distinguished from game ranching by its "greater intensity of management reflected most tangibly by the transport of live animals to auctions or slaughter facilities." The majority of the Canadian wildlife industry is composed of private operations, and is therefore not included in the spectrum of community-based wildlife management activities.

The number of Aboriginal game farming/ranching projects has increased significantly in the last twenty years. This increase is due mainly to two factors:

- changes in provincial legislation that promote game farming as a means of diversification of agriculture and thereby create the necessary legislative and economic infrastructure; and,
- an overall revival of traditional values among Canada's Aboriginal people.

Wildlife management is largely a provincial matter and laws and regulations dealing with commercial wildlife production differ widely among provinces. Generally, only species native to a province at the time wildlife legislation was enacted are considered wildlife and subject to regulation. In the past ten years, a number of provinces have enacted 'livestock diversification' acts which transfer responsibility for administering the industry from wildlife to agriculture departments and lift the strict prohibitions on commercial sale of wildlife products. Legislation in each province typically treats native and exotic species differently.

Native species commonly ranched in Canada are:

- bison—including plains bison (*Bison bison bison*) and wood bison (*Bison bison athabascae*)
- wapiti (elk) (*Cervus elaphus canadensis*)
- white-tailed deer (*Odocoileus virginianus*)

Mule deer (*Odocoileus hemionus*) and moose (*Alces alces*) have proven difficult to farm and are not widespread. Red deer (*Cervus elaphus elaphus*), fallow deer (*Dama dama*), reindeer (*Rangifer tarandus tarandus*) and wild boar (*Sus scrofa*) are the most common non-native species.

With the exception of reindeer, Aboriginal communities tend to ranch native species, especially wapiti and bison. In Alberta and Manitoba, Aboriginal groups are in the process of establishing herds from wood bison populations, an activity which most likely falls into the spectrum of co-management (see Chapter 1). On Banks Island (NWT), the local muskox population has increased to the edge of carrying capacity, creating a rather intensive management system, whereas some reindeer projects evolved from family-owned herds into corporate ownership of large free-roaming herds. As these examples may illustrate, it is difficult to draw a distinct line between game farming in a conventional agro-economic sense, and co-management projects when dealing with the topic of game farming amongst Aboriginal Canadians.

Due to the scarcity of data available and the diversity of Aboriginal game production approaches, this paper is far from claiming to present a complete survey of the present situation. Instead, it should be seen as an overview of the different aspects of game farming among Canadian Aboriginal communities. Examples are drawn from non-native species (reindeer) and native species (wapiti and bison) to illustrate the current status and development of this facet of community-based wildlife management in Canada.

Status of game ranching among Canada's Aboriginal people

5.1 History of Aboriginal game ranching

Historically, the Aboriginal inhabitants of Canada were hunting and gathering people who strongly relied on wildlife for food, clothing, shelter, and other aspects of life. Other than dogs, the domestication of animals was never part of the pre-European lifestyle. However, with the arrival of the Spanish-introduced horse (about 1750 in western Canada), many Aboriginal groups, especially of the prairies, soon became skilled horse owners and breeders. Many tribes owned large herds and the use of fast horses made bison hunts more successful. With the extirpation of the large free-roaming bison herds of North America and the loss of their former land base, many former bison-hunting Aboriginal peoples started cattle operations on their reserve lands.

Over the years, Federal, Provincial, and Territorial governments have acknowledged the special relationship of Native people to wildlife by encouraging various game farming/herding operations. On the other hand, other government decisions threaten these special relationships, as in the cases of diseased wood bison in Wood Buffalo National Park and a continued forestry interest in the wood bison release range of the Waterhen wood bison herd in Manitoba (Stock 1996).

5.2 Open doors and barriers in provincial legislation

The status of game farming across Canada depends heavily on provincial legislation, which varies considerably. Alberta, for example, only allows farming of native species (the recent exception being a small number of reindeer) in contrast to Manitoba, where until recently only non-native species could be farmed. British Columbia allows the farming of fallow deer, reindeer, and bison.

Theoretically, Indian bands are, to a certain degree, exempt from provincial legislation because their reservation lands were established via treaties with the Crown, and these lands fall under federal jurisdiction. This status is an advantage only as long as a tribal group chooses to undertake game farming for subsistence purposes only. As soon as an Indian band tries to trade or exchange game or game products outside a reservation, provincial legislation applies. Every transaction that is not within provincial laws must therefore be classified as illegal or subject to further arrangements with the respective provincial government. However, in cases of cooperation between Aboriginal groups and a provincial government. Treaty status can give advantages to Aboriginal people that are not available to the general public. Most provinces offer Aboriginal people priority access to surplus stock taken from public lands.

5.3 Game farming of non-native species: reindeer herding

The reindeer is the Eurasian domesticated equivalent of the wild North American caribou. A well-established and long-standing reindeer industry on the Seward Peninsula, Alaska does not have a counterpart in Canada. Reindeer have been introduced to various parts of the Canadian north and these reindeer operations share a story of mixed success. As an introduced species, the reindeer has continued to be of local importance to at least two Canadian Arctic Aboriginal communities: Tuktoyaktuk, NWT and Sanikiluaq, Nunavut[26]. The idea of introducing domesticated reindeer into the Native American lifestyle originated in Alaska at the end of the last century and was promoted by missionaries and teachers such as Sheldon Jackson. One aim of this introduction was to supply remote northern communities with a reliable source of food. Another was to try to assimilate Native Americans to a more Western lifestyle by trying to introduce the herding system of Native Scandinavians. This idea made its way to Canada in the 1930s where the first herds, from Alaska, were introduced. At least five attempts were made to develop commercial reindeer ventures, of which only the Mackenzie Delta herd is still operating.

The original idea of reindeer herding was to establish a government-owned main herd, from which small herds were to be given to interested Inuit so they could establish their own herds. Once these herds increased in size, the Inuit owners were to repay the number of animals they obtained from the main herd (Scotter 1972, 1989; Notzke 1994). The project never reached its intended goal, although six family-owned herds were established between 1938 and 1954. After some years of growth, there was a period of decline, after which the herds returned to government ownership. A number of different explanations have been put forward to account for this development. The decline in reindeer numbers, for example, might be

---

26. Sanikiluaq was part of the NWT until the creation of Nunavut on April 1, 1999.

attributed to the fact that the domesticated reindeer are herded in the same area year-round. The short arctic summer only allows a brief period for vegetation growth that might, over the years, lead to a shortage in food. Free-roaming caribou would simply migrate to other places, whereas the reindeer remained in one place. The failure to introduce modern management practices and a general lack of interest among local Aboriginal people are probably major reasons for the failure of this experiment (see Notzke 1994).

In 1974, the Federal Government sold the entire Mackenzie Delta reindeer herd to a privately-owned company, Canadian Reindeer Ltd., owned in succession by two local people from Tuktoyaktuk, NWT. The owners were able to turn the operation into a million-dollar-a-year enterprise (Notzke 1994). This financial success was achieved by securing access to both the southern meat market and the oriental antler market. The economic potential of this reindeer operation is now in question because of the settlement of a comprehensive claim in the Western Arctic. The *Inuvialuit Final Agreement* (IFA) turned the (essentially free) grazing grounds of Canadian Reindeer Ltd. into private Inuvialuit land. To date, there has been no resolution of the status of the reindeer herd that is acceptable to both the current owners of the herd and the new land owners.

Quite a different example of Aboriginal use of introduced reindeer comes from the community of Sanikiluaq on the Belcher Islands, Nunavut. Due to severe weather conditions, native caribou disappeared from these islands in Hudson Bay in the late 1800s. In 1978, the Government of the Northwest Territories introduced reindeer to the Belcher Islands with the long-term aim of supplementing the traditional Inuit diet of predominantly marine foods (McDonald and Fleming 1991). The Belcher Islands reindeer are now free-roaming and are managed by the local Inuit through the harvest of a certain number of animals per year. This form of use is closer to community wildlife management than to herding.

Herding of wild caribou is currently being explored in northern Quebec as a community enterprise (see Chapter 3). This experiment is being watched with interest because caribou are more difficult to manage than reindeer.

5.4 Game ranching of native species: wapiti and bison

Most Canadian Aboriginal groups prefer low-input extensive game ranching with a minimum of interference with their animals. This approach can likely be attributed to a cultural value system that differs from the western management system. In the United States, this conclusion has become evident with the formation of the Inter Tribal Bison Cooperative (ITBC) in 1991. The ITBC's mission statement is:

> *"To restore bison to Indian Nations in a manner which is compatible with our spiritual and cultural beliefs and practices."*
> —(ITBC 1996).

At the present time, it is difficult to make statements applicable to the situation in all of Canada. However, in May 1996, the Manitoba First Nations Elk and Bison Council (MFNEBC) was formed and currently has 17 Manitoba Aboriginal groups as members (Payne 1998). The main goals of the MFNEBC are as follows:

> *"To establish healthy and prosperous game farming units in Manitoba First Nations, through the development and enhancement of business, economic development, and employment in First Nations in a culturally appropriate way."*—(Payne 1997:6,12).

Wapiti (Elk) Farming—The current success of the Canadian wapiti industry is based on production of antler velvet for the traditional oriental medicine markets in Korea, Hong Kong, and Taiwan (Hudson and Burton 1993). Especially in the prairie provinces, a number of Indian bands have started elk operations. The production aims vary considerably among the different bands. Some are involved in antler velvet production, whereas others focus on the production of breeding stock due to opposition in their communities toward antler harvest.

The demand for breeding stock is strong and prices for individual breeding females range from $10,000-$25,000. A premium is paid for tame animals with well-documented bloodlines and performance records. This, along with the need for disease testing, requires herds to be managed rather intensively.

Elk ranching was pioneered in Alberta by the Métis community of Kikino. Their large enclosure (approximately nine sections)[27] was stocked initially with surplus animals from Elk Island National Park. They originally envisaged an extensive production system based on

---

26. One section of land = 640 acres.

Status of game ranching among Canada's Aboriginal people

guided hunts and field slaughter, but high prices encouraged them to enter the breeding stock market.

Some interesting recent developments in the Province of Manitoba may give an insight into the potential of this sector among Canadian Aboriginal communities. Until recently, Manitoba allowed game farming only of non-native species. In 1996, the Manitoba government passed new legislation, *The Livestock Industry Diversification and Consequential Amendments Act*. The province also created a new programme known as the "Elk Seedstock Program for the Game Farming Industry." The purpose of this programme is to enable prospective Manitoba elk farmers to more easily establish new operations in the currently high-priced Canadian elk industry. Over a three-year period, approximately 250 elk are to be captured from the provinces' major wild herds (Payne 1997, 1998). Prospective farmers can purchase these elk on a draw basis at prices below current market value. Many Manitoba Aboriginal groups expressed early interest in elk farming and undertook negotiations with the Provincial Government that led to the *First Nations—Province of Manitoba Elk Farming Alliance Agreement*. This agreement actively involves Aboriginal communities in the elk capture programme, which is supervised and coordinated by the MFNEBC. The *Elk Farming Alliance Agreement* will result in the establishment of a captive source herd, from which animals will be distributed to Indian bands to start their own operations. The MFNEBC

Figure 7. *Elk. Some farming operations focus on antler velvet production. Photo by R.Hudson.*

will distribute elk to interested bands after consideration of the following factors:

- political and financial stability;
- business experience/success;
- condition of the proposed facility;
- training or potential qualification of managers/employees.

The MFNEBC also provides training and research programs as well as consultation for its members (Payne 1997). This professional approach, adopted to establish prosperous game farming units on Manitoba Indian lands in accordance with cultural values, has a high potential for success. Creation of their own council might help Manitoba bands establish their operations much faster than Aboriginal operations in other provinces that were started at a time when the industry was still in its infancy.

Bison Ranching—In most provinces, the plains bison (*Bison bison bison*) is not regarded as wildlife, but rather as domestic livestock and therefore does not fall under the responsibility of provincial fish and wildlife administration. The status of the wood bison subspecies (*Bison bison athabascae*) is somewhat different because this subspecies is classified as "threatened" by the Committee on the Status of Endangered Wildlife in Canada (COSEWIC), and was recently downlisted from "Appendix I" to "Appendix II" by the Convention on International Trade in Endangered Species (CITES). These classifications tend to limit farming or ranching opportunities, especially in provinces that regard the wood bison as wildlife.

Despite these restrictions, the Waterhen Wood Bison Project in Manitoba serves as a good example of a cooperative undertaking between Native bands and a provincial government for the benefit of both Native people and an endangered species. The Waterhen Wood Bison Project started in 1983-84, when 34 wood bison that were considered surplus stock were brought to Waterhen from several Canadian sources, including zoological parks and gardens, and Elk Island National Park (Payne *et al.* 1993, Stock 1996). These animals were kept in a compound and became seedstock for a commercial as well as a wild herd. In March 1991, 13 wood bison that were reared in and imprinted upon the region were released north of the Waterhen settlement to establish a free-roaming herd. Formation of a commercial herd was also part of this project. Wood bison tend to be larger than plains bison and are therefore sought after in the bison breeding business. The Waterhen Wood Bison Project is regarded as successful in establishing a free-roaming wood bison herd (Payne et al. 1993, Stock 1996). As one among several wood bison projects in Canada, this one helped in the down-listing of the wood bison from 'endangered' to 'threatened'. Payne et al. (1993) also noted that this project resulted in the revival of old skills (like tanning) which otherwise might soon have been lost to the Waterhen community.

Figure 8. *Bison. Photo by L. Carbyn (CCI Archives).*

Another interesting development concerning Aboriginal communities and their access to publicly-owned bison is the distribution of surplus animals from Elk Island National Park in Alberta. This park is small and supports one of the largest densities of hoofed mammals in the world. Until the 1960s, surplus bison from the park were killed and the meat distributed to Aboriginal communities in Alberta. After a number of requests from these communities to obtain live animals, in 1967 the Park started donating surplus bison to Aboriginal bands. Elk Island National Park's current policy is to donate at least six calves per year to Aboriginal communities that wish to establish bison herds for cultural purposes. The band obtaining the animals pays only the costs of their handling. The success of these community-based bison operations is mixed. At least one operation was given up after some years, due to internal band politics and rivalries. Others, like the Alexander Band and the Kikino Métis Settlement, have established successful ranching businesses.

5.5 Conclusions and outlook for the future

The subject of game farming and ranching among Canada's Aboriginal people is as diverse as the communities and game species involved. To date in Canada, success of these operations has been mixed. Based on the limited available data, it can be concluded that Canadian Aboriginal communities prefer ranching of native game species that were traditionally hunted (like wapiti) and/or are of high cultural significance (like bison). These species can be ranched very successfully if an overall market exists for meat or other products. The rapid growth of membership in the ITBC in the United States might be indicative of the potential that game ranching has among Aboriginal communities when the concept is implemented in accordance with cultural values. ITBC reports indicate that the return of the bison to Aboriginal settlements awakens a revival of traditional values, knowledge, and pride.

There also appears to be a tendency among many Aboriginal game farming/ranching operations to manage the animals in a more natural and extensive way than many private (non-Aboriginal) producers. Aboriginal bison ranchers, for example, often refuse to implement common management practices like dehorning/velveting or finishing animals in feedlots. Although these practices might result in loss of financial opportunities, benefits might be gained through communal identification with the operation and a revival of cultural values associated with the animals. The potential impact of these Aboriginal producers on meat and velvet markets that target environmental and health-conscious customers could be a topic of future interest.

The provincial livestock diversification acts were based on the expectation that animals would be used for agricultural purposes. However, pressure is mounting to enable paid hunts on fenced properties. In Saskatchewan, this is allowed as an extension of a provision for on-farm slaughter. Although there always has been considerable public resistance to paid hunting in Canada, other provinces may follow Saskatchewan. Already, many senior stags and bucks are sold to hunt ranches in the United States. The reaction to this development is mixed, but it does mean that animals will be managed more extensively and perhaps more humanely. Aboriginal communities have expressed some interest in this hunt market and some see opportunities for guided hunts on their large communal land bases.

It must be noted that game ranching still stirs debate in Canada. Opponents of the practice voice numerous concerns, including dangers

Status of game ranching among Canada's Aboriginal people

to wild populations, privatization of public resources, and impacts on genetic resources (see Geist 1995a, b). Breed 'improvement' is a natural extension of efforts to maximize market value for breeding stock. Bison have perhaps been spared the frenzy that surrounds the wapiti industry, where artificial insemination has been adapted as a standard practice to breed stags with superior antlers. A natural consequence is the demand to introduce genes of Asian wapiti, whose antlers are esteemed on Korean markets. These trends certainly conflict with the original concepts of game farming that viewed the industry as a means to conserve the variety of native game species (Telfer and Scotter 1975). In 1990, the Indian Association of Alberta opposed the government's planned legalization of this practice, viewing it as a threat to both wildlife resources and Native hunting rights (*Windspeaker*, cited in Notzke 1994). However, claims of illegal dealings and other negative effects failed to materialize, and did not seem to influence the eagerness of communities to consider these ventures.

Despite initial concerns, game ranching is now a well-established branch of Canadian agriculture. In agricultural areas, game ranching may offer opportunities to maintain both sustainable agriculture and wildlife habitat (Hudson 1995). On both agricultural and more marginal lands, some Canadian Aboriginal communities are successfully supplementing their community income through game farming and ranching operations. For the future, there is a large potential for combining game ranching with other income-generating activities, including ecotourism and sport hunting. The 21st century is likely to bring even more diversity in both species and activities related to game ranching in Canada's Aboriginal communities.

CHAPTER 6:

Reflections on Canadian experience in community-based wildlife management

Leslie Treseder

Conclusions that can be drawn from the Canadian experience in community-based wildlife management are based on other regional reviews for the 'Evaluating Eden' project and comments on the first draft of this report. Major conclusions applicable to the 'Evaluating Eden' project fall into four main categories:

- recognition of Aboriginal land use;
- need for capacity-building;
- importance of subsistence hunting to northern community economies;
- long-term viability of community-based wildlife management.

Recognition of Aboriginal Land Use—Despite more than a century of concerted assimilation policy, Canada's northern Aboriginal people have not been 'assimilated' into the larger (Euro-Canadian) society. Canada's northern Aboriginal people have depended and will continue to depend on wildlife for cultural and economic survival. There has been increasing recognition of the importance of Aboriginal land use in northern Canada, as well as increasing acknowledgement of Aboriginal rights to wildlife. In the context of comprehensive claims, Aboriginal wildlife rights are protected by both claims settlement legislation and the Canadian Constitution. This type of legislative recognition evolved over a relatively short period of time and offers hope to other communities seeking security of tenure in access to wildlife resources.

Need for Capacity-Building—Each chapter in this report identifies various institutional and other barriers to implementation of community-based wildlife management. There is a need for capacity-building at all levels, including communities, governments, academia, industry, and other stakeholders. All parties involved in wildlife management need to work together to build effective relationships and institutions which facilitate implementation of community-based wildlife management initiatives.

Importance of Subsistence Hunting to Northern Community Economics—The economies of most northern Canadian communities will continue to be based on a mix of domestic (subsistence) production, wage employment, enterprise, and transfer payments for the foreseeable future. Much work has been done on valuation of the non-market economics of subsistence, and subsistence activities are recognized as a cornerstone of the mixed northern economy.

Figure 9. *Porcupine Caribou Management Board Meeting. Photo by M. Ivanitz (CCI archives).*

Subsistence is a viable land use option for the twenty-first century and a preferred source of livelihood for some northern community residents. Protection of subsistence land use increases the number of options available as part of the mixed northern economy. There is a great deal of interest in preserving subsistence as a future land use

Reflections on Canadian Experience

option, regardless of the number of people actually engaged in this activity. Subsistence harvesting rights are recognized in some protected areas in the Canadian north, and subsistence hunting can be compatible with protected area management objectives in remote areas. For the future, there is great potential for more involvement of northern Aboriginal communities in the management of protected areas.

There are many challenges associated with the maintenance of subsistence harvesting as a future land use option, not the least of which is the growing number of people dependent on the resource base. As the example in Chapter 2 of this paper illustrates, however, there can be a stable harvest of wildlife in communities with high population growth, due to a stable or declining number of people on the land pursuing subsistence activities. Maintenance of subsistence harvesting also requires effective community self-regulation, as well as protection from potentially conflicting land uses. Community-based wildlife management systems are vulnerable to both social and environmental impacts associated with industrial development. Social impacts include changes to local institutions and the ability of communities to maintain systems for regulation and allocation of harvesting. Maintaining these community-based systems will be a critical challenge for Canada's northern Aboriginal people in the twenty-first century.

Long-term Viability of Community-Based Wildlife Management
—Community-based wildlife management offers many opportunities to contribute to social, cultural, and economic development in remote communities. Wildlife-based options for supporting community economic development depend on factors such as the available land base, community access to resources, and the status of the local resource base. Appropriate scale is a critical (and common) element in all of the wildlife-based activities discussed in this report. Recognizing that subsistence harvesting is the first priority for community use of wildlife resources, other wildlife-based options for community economic development include commercial hunting, tourism, and game ranching.

Commercial hunting of wildlife must be well-planned in order to avoid negative impacts on subsistence harvesting. Where the resource base can support both subsistence and commercial harvesting, commercial activities can be compatible with both conservation and community development objectives. Commercial hunting can also have social/cultural as well as economic benefits.

Wildlife-based tourism, particularly big game sport hunting, is currently thought to be compatible with northern Aboriginal lifestyles/cultures. Ecotourism has a vast, largely untapped potential and represents a major economic opportunity for the future. Like commercial harvesting, ecotourism must be carefully planned to minimize disruption of subsistence harvesting activities and other aspects of life in northern communities. Education of tourists and local operators will be critical to the future success of ecotourism in the Canadian north.

Figure 10. *Hunting caribou off the west coast of Hudson Bay. Photo by M. Freeman (ca. 1961).*

Game ranching offers a number of opportunities for both economic development and cultural revitalization, especially for communities with limited land bases. Game ranching overlaps with other sectors in the wildlife-based economy, including subsistence hunting (as a source of meat for community residents), commercial hunting (sale of meat and other products to export markets) and tourism (both sport hunting and wildlife viewing). Game ranching is likely to play an important role in the future economies of some communities in the Canadian north.

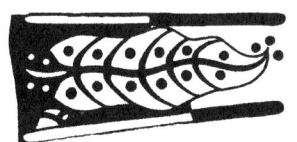

References

Adventure Travel Society. 1994. *Adventure Travel Society Newsletter.*

Alberta Native Affairs. 1986. *The Concept and Nature of Aboriginal Rights: An Overview.* Edmonton: Policy and Planning Branch, Native Affairs Secretariat, Background Paper No. 2.

Aylward, K. 1997. Ministerial statement—commercial caribou license issues. Department of Forest Resources and Agrifoods. St. John's: Government of Newfoundland and Labrador, December 4, 1997.

Bailey, J., N.B. Snow, A. Carpenter, and L. Carpenter. 1995.Cooperative Wildlife Management under the Western Arctic Inuvialuit Land Claim, pp. 11-15 in Bissonette, J.A., and P.R. Krausman (eds.), *Integrating People and Wildlife for a Sustainable Future.* Proceedings of the First International Wildlife Management Congress. Bethesda: The Wildlife Society.

Barnston, G. 1861. Recollections of the swans and geese of Hudson's Bay. *Canadian Naturalist and Geologist* **6:** 337-344.

Beaudoin, T. 1990. *Report on Spring 1990 Muskox Harvest at Sachs Harbour, Banks Island, NWT.* Inuvik: Inuvialuit Game Council; prepared for NWT Department of Economic Development and Tourism, 13p.

Bennett, D. 1982. *Subsistence v. Commercial Use: The Meaning of these Words in Relation to Hunting and Fishing by Canada's Native Peoples.* Ottawa: Canadian Arctic Resources Committee, Working Paper No. 3,

Berger, T.R. 1977. *Northern Frontier, Northern Homeland. The Report of the Mackenzie Valley Pipeline Inquiry, Volume II.* Ottawa: Supply and Services Canada.

Berkes, F. 1997. New and not-so-new directions in the use of the commons: Co-Management. *Common Property Resource Digest* **42:** 5-7.

Berkes, F. 1994. Co-management: bridging the two solitudes. *Northern Perspectives* **22(2-3):** 18-20.

Berkes, F., and T. Henley. 1997. Co-management and traditional knowledge: Threat or opportunity? *Policy Options* **March 1997:** 29-31.

Berkes, F., and H. Fast. 1996. Aboriginal peoples: The basis for policy-making towards sustainable development, pp. 204-264 in Dale, A., and J.B. Robinson (eds.), *Achieving Sustainable Development.* Vancouver: University of British Columbia Press.

Berkes, F., P.J. George, R.J. Preston, A. Hughes, J. Turner, and B.D. Cummins. 1994. Wildlife harvesting and sustainable regional Native economy in the Hudson and James Bay Lowland, Ontario. *Arctic* **47:** 350-360.

Berkes, F., P. George, and R.J. Preston. 1991. Co-management: the evolution in theory and practice of the joint administration of living resources. *Alternatives* **18:** 12-18.

Berkes, F., D. Feeny, B.J. McCay, and J.M. Acheson. 1989. The benefits of the commons. Commentary. *Nature* **340:** 91-93.

Bishop, C.A., and T. Morantz (eds.). 1986. Who owns the beaver? Algonquian land tenure reconsidered. Special issue of *Anthropologica* **28(1-2)**.

Brightman, R.A. 1993. *Grateful Prey. Rocky Cree Human-Animal Relationships.* Berkeley: University of California Press.

Brody, H. 1981. *Maps and Dreams.* Vancouver: Douglas and McIntyre.

Bufo Incorporated. 1992a. *1992 Western Arctic Visitor Survey. Preliminary Analysis.* Vancouver: Bufo Incorporated, submitted to GNWT Department of Economic Development and Tourism.

Bufo Incorporated. 1992b. *1992 Western Arctic Visitor Survey. Summary Report.* Vancouver: Bufo Incorporated, submitted to GNWT Department of Economic Development and Tourism.

Burt, P.M. *et al.* 1993. A course for teachers about the Arctic in the Arctic. *Information North* **19(3):** 1-8.

Butler, E. 1990. An ecotourist in Bathurst Inlet. *Borealis* **1(4):** 42-46.

Caughley, G. 1977. *Analysis of Vertebrate Populations.* London: John Wiley and Sons, 234p.

Caughley, G., and A. Gunn. 1996. Chapter 11: Economics and Trade pp. 341-374 in Caughley, G., and A. Gunn (eds.), *Conservation Biology in Theory and Practice.* Cambridge, Massachusetts: Blackwell Science.

Caughley, G., and A. Gunn. 1993. Dynamics of large herbivores in deserts: kangaroos and caribou. *Oikos* **67:** 47-55.

Clark, C.W. 1991. Economic biases against sustainable development, pp. 319-330 in Costanza, R. (ed.), *Ecological Economics: The Science and Management of Sustainability.* New York: Columbia University Press.

Colford, J. 1998. *Background of the NWT Food and Meat Industry.* Yellowknife: Department of Resources, Wildlife, and Economic Development. GNWT Departmental Report.

Conrad, J.M. 1989. Bioeconomics and the bowhead whale. *Journal of Political Economy* **97:** 974-987.

Daniel, R.C. 1980. *A History of Native Claims Processes in Canada 1867-1979.* Ottawa: Prepared by Tyler, Wright & Daniel Ltd. for the Department of Indian and Northern Affairs Research Branch, 248p.

Department of Indian Affairs and Northern Development. 1990. *The Canadian Indian.* Ottawa: Minister of Supply and Services Canada.

Department of Indian Affairs and Northern Development. 1986. *Comprehensive Land Claims Policy.* Ottawa: Minister of Supply and Services Canada.

Department of Renewable Resources (NWT). 1994. *Tradition and Change. A Strategy for Renewable Resource Development in the Northwest Territories.* Yellowknife: Government of the Northwest Territories, 23p.

Derek Murray Consulting Associates, The North Group, and Norecon Ltd. 1994. *Northwest Territories Tourism Marketing Strategy 1994-95—1998-99.*

References

Yellowknife: Prepared for GNWT Department of Economic Development and Tourism.

Drolet, C.A., A. Reed, M. Breton, and F. Berkes. 1987. Sharing wildlife management responsibilities with Native groups: case histories in Northern Quebec, pp. 389-398 in: *Transactions of the Fifty-Second North American Wildlife and Natural Resources Conference.* Washington, D.C.: Wildlife Management Institute, SK 351N86.

Doubleday, N. 1989. Co-management provisions of the Inuvialuit Final Agreement, pp. 209-227 in Pinkerton, E. (ed.), *Cooperative Management of Local Fisheries: New Directions for Improved Management and Community Development.* Vancouver: University of British Columbia Press.

Elias, P.D. 1995. Northern economies, pp. 3-35 in Elias, P.D. (ed.), *Northern Aboriginal Communities: Economies and Development.* North York: Captus University Publications.

Elias, P.D. 1989. Aboriginal rights and litigation: history and future of court decisions in Canada. *Polar Record* **25(152):** 1-8.

Epler-Wood, M. 1997. New directions in the ecotourism industry. *The Ecotourist Society Newsletter* **First Quarter:** 1-3

Feit, H.A. 1991. Gifts of the land: Hunting territories, guaranteed incomes, and the construction of social relations in James Bay Cree society. *Senri Ethnological Studies* **30:** 223-268.

Fisheries Joint Management Committee (FJMC). 1991. *Beaufort Sea Beluga Management Plan.* Inuvik: FJMC.

Fournier, B., and A. Gunn. 1997. *Muskox Numbers and Distribution in the Northwest Territories.* Yellowknife: NWT Resources, Wildlife and Economic Development File Report.

Freeman, M.M.R. 1997. Issues affecting subsistence security in arctic societies. *Arctic Anthropology* **34(1):** 7-17.

Freeman, M.M.R. 1993. The International Whaling Commission, small type whaling, and coming to terms with subsistence. *Human Organization* **52:** 243-251.

Freeman, M.M.R. 1986. Renewable resources, economics, and Native communities, pp. 29-37 in *Native People and Renewable Resource Management.* The 1986 Symposium of the Alberta Society of Professional Biologists, 29 April-1 May 1986. Edmonton: Alberta Society of Professional Biologists.

Freeman, M.M.R. 1984. Contemporary Inuit exploitation of sea-ice environments, pp. 73-96 in Cooke, A, and E. Van Alstine (eds.), *Sikumiut: People Who Use the Sea-ice.* Ottawa: Canadian Arctic Resources Committee.

Freeman, M.M.R. (ed.). 1976. *Report of the Inuit Land Use and Occupancy Project.* Three Volumes. Ottawa: Department of Indian and Northern Affairs.

Freeman, M.M.R., and L.N. Carbyn (eds.). 1988. *Traditional Knowledge and Renewable Resource Management in Northern Regions.* Edmonton: Canadian Circumpolar Institute, Occasional Publication No. 23.

Freeman, M.M.R., E.E. Wein, and D.E. Keith. 1992. *Recovering Rights: Bowhead Whales and Inuvialuit Subsistence in the Western Canadian*

Arctic. Edmonton: Canadian Circumpolar Institute, Occasional Publication 31.

Geist, V. 1995a. Wildlife conservation American style creates biodiversity and wealth, pp. 279-282 in Bisonnette, J.A., and P.R. Krausman (eds.), *Integrating People and Wildlife for a Sustainable Future.* Proceedings of the First International Wildlife Management Congress. Bethesda, Maryland: The Wildlife Society.

Geist, V. 1995b. North American policies of wildlife conservation, pp. 77-129 in Geist, V., and I. McTaggart-Cowan (eds.), *Wildlife Conservation Policy: A Reader.* Calgary: Detselig Enterprises Ltd.

George, P., and R.J. Preston. 1987. "Going in between": The impact of European technology on the work patterns of the West Main Cree of Northern Ontario. *Journal of Economic History* **47**: 447-460.

Government of the Northwest Territories (GNWT). 1995. *1995 NWT Exit Survey. General report on visitors to the Northwest Territories.* Yellowknife: GNWT, Economic Planning Section, Policy, Planning & Human Resources.

GNWT. 1983. *Community-Based Tourism. A Strategy for the Northwest Territories Tourism Industry.* Yellowknife: GNWT Department of Economic Development and Tourism.

Grekin, J., and S. Milne. 1996. Toward sustainable tourism development: the case of Pond Inlet, NWT, pp. 76-106 in Butler, R., and T. Hinch (eds.), *Tourism and Indigenous Peoples.* Toronto: International Thomson Business Press.

Gunn, A. 1998. Personal communication. Ungulate biologist, Department of Resources, Wildlife, and Economic Development, Government of the Northwest Territories, Yellowknife, NWT.

Gunn, A., J. Adamczewski, and B. Elkin. 1991. Commercial harvesting of muskoxen in the Northwest Territories, pp. 197-203 in Renecker, L.A., and R.J. Hudson (eds.), *Wildlife Production: Conservation and Sustainable Development.* Fairbanks: University of Alaska.

Hamilton, A.C. 1995. *Canada and Aboriginal Peoples: A New Partnership.* Report of Hon A.C. Hamilton, Fact Finder for Minister of Indian Affairs and Northern Development. Ottawa: Minister of Public Works and Government Services.

Howard, A. and Widdowson. 1997. Traditional knowledge advocates weave a tangled web. *Policy Options* **April:** 46-48.

Hardin, G. 1968. The tragedy of the commons. *Science* **162**: 1243-1248.

Haugh, A. 1994. Balancing rights, powers, and privileges: a window on co-management experience in Manitoba. *Northern Perspectives* **22(2-3)**: 28-32.

Howard, A., and F. Widdowson. 1996. Traditional knowledge threatens environmental assessment. *Policy Options* **November**: 34-36.

Hudson, R.J. 1996. International deer industry. *Canadian Elk and Deer Farmer.*

Hudson, R.J. 1995. Wildlife ranching: dancing with the devil? pp. 223-232 in Geist, V., and I. McTaggart-Cowan (eds.). *Wildlife Conservation Policy: A Reader.* Calgary: Detselig Enterprises Ltd.

References

Hudson, R.J., and B.A. Burton. 1993. The wildlife industry, in Martin, J., R.J. Hudson, and B.A. Young (eds.), *Animal Production in Canada*. Edmonton.

Hudson, R.J., and D.H.M. Cumming. 1989. Recreational and commercial hunting, pp. 113-114 in Hudson, R.J., K.R. Drew, and L.M. Baskin (eds.), *Wildlife Production Systems: Economic Utilization of Wild Ungulates*. Cambridge, Mass.: Cambridge University Press.

Idyll, C.P. 1973. The anchovy crisis. *Scientific American* **228**: 22.

Indian Claims Commission. 1975. *Indian claims in Canada: an introductory essay and selected list of library holdings*. Ottawa: Information Canada.

Inter Tribal Bison Cooperative (ITBC). 1996. *Annual Report 1994-95*. Rapid City, South Dakota.

Inuvialuit Communications Society (ICS). 1995a. *Tusaayaksat* **11(29)**, July 28, 1995.

Inuvialuit Communications Society (ICS). 1995b. *Nutakaptingnun Qimaksavut: Our Children's Legacy*. Inuvik: ICS Video Produced for Parks Canada.

Inuvialuit Game Council. (IGC) 1994. *Tourism Guidelines Within the Inuvialuit Settlement Region*. Approved by the Inuvialuit Game Council, June 22, 1994.

Jenks, B. 1997. The question of local guides in Latin America. *The Ecotourism Society Newsletter* **Second Quarter**: 1-2.

Jingfors, K. 1986. Inuit harvesting levels of caribou in the Kitikmeot Region, Northwest Territories, Canada, 1982-1984. *Rangifer* **Special Issue No. 1**: 167-172.

Keith, R. 1993. The MCB Workshops: Reflections on co-management. *Northern Perspectives* **21(2)**: 13-15.

Kelsall, J.P. 1968. *The Migratory Barren-Ground Caribou of Canada*. Ottawa: Canadian Wildlife Service, Monograph No. 3, 340p.

Klein, D.R. 1989. Northern subsistence hunting economies, pp. 96-111 in Hudson, R.J., K.R. Drew, and L.M. Baskin (eds.), *Wildlife Production Systems: Economic Utilization of Wild Ungulates*. Cambridge: Cambridge University Press.

Kothari, A., R.V. Anuradha, and N. Pathak. 1997. *Community-Based Conservation: Issues and Prospects*. Paper for presentation at the Regional Workshop on Community-Based Conservation Policy and Practice, New Delhi, India, 9-11 February 1997.

Krieg, K.L. 1989. Strategies for marketing game meats, pp. 538-542 in Hudson, R.J., K.R. Drew, and L.M. Baskin (eds.), *Wildlife Production Systems: Economic Utilization of Wild Ungulates*. Cambridge: Cambridge University Press.

Leader-Williams, N. 1988. *Reindeer on South Georgia. The Ecology of an Introduced Population*. Cambridge: Cambridge University Press.

Leboubon, D. 1998. Personal communication. Regional Wildlife Manager, Department of Forest Resources and Agrifoods, Government of Newfoundland & Labrador, February 2, 1998.

Lowi, E. 1997. Track 'em down, round 'em up, herd 'em in, rawhide. *Canadian Geographic* **May/June**: 72-78.

MacDonald, T. 1993. Ecotourism and indigenous people: from endangered species to resource managers. *Tour & Travel News* **Supplement Oct. 25**: 12-15.

MacLachlan, L. 1994. Co-management of wildlife in northern Aboriginal comprehensive land-claim agreements. *Northern Perspectives* **22(2-3)**: 21-27.

Mackenzie, D. 1995. The cod that disappeared. *New Scientist* **Sept.**: 25-29.

Makowecki, R. 1993. *Treaty Indian Hunting and Fishing in Alberta*. Edmonton: Alberta Environmental Protection, Fish and Wildlife Services. Background Paper, Three volumes.

McCay, B.J., and J.M. Acheson (eds.). 1987. *The Question of the Commons: The Culture and Ecology of Communal Resources*. Tuscon: University of Arizona Press.

McDonald, M., and B. Fleming. 1991. *The Role of Traditional Knowledge in Community-Based Management of an Eiderdown Industry Developing in Northern Canada*. Paper presented at the International Association for the Study of Common Property (IASCP) Conference, 26-29 September, Winnipeg, Manitoba, Canada.

Merlino, D. 1993. Ecotourism. Past, present, and future. *Tour & Travel News* **Supplement Oct. 25**: 4-5.

Moss, J. 1994. Engineering wilderness. *Arctic Circle* **Spring**: 10-13, 22-27.

Murray, A.R. 1995. *Involvement of Aboriginal People in Environmental and Renewable Resource Management in Canada*. Regina: Alan Murray & Associates, prepared for Saskatchewan Environment and Resource Management. Two Volumes.

National Research Council (NRC). 1986. *Proceedings of the Conference on Common Property Resource Management*. Washington: National Academy Press.

Noss. R.F. 1995. *Maintaining Ecological Integrity in Representative Resource Networks*. Ottawa: World Wildlife Fund, discussion paper, 77p.

Notzke, C. 1995a. A new perspective in Aboriginal natural resource management: co-management. *Geoforum* **26(2)**: 187-209.

Notzke, C. 1995b. *Aboriginal Tourism Development in the Western Arctic*. Lethbridge: University of Lethbridge, unpublished research report.

Notzke, C. 1994. *Aboriginal Peoples and Natural Resources in Canada*. North York: Captus University Publications.

Notzke, C. 1993. Aboriginal peoples and natural resources: co-management, the way of the future? *National Geographic Research and Exploration* **9(4)**: 395-397.

NWT Legislative Assembly. 1989. *Special committee on the northern economy (SCONE)*. Yellowknife: Legislative Assembly of the Northwest Territories, 76p.

Ohmagari, K., and F. Berkes. 1997. Transmission of indigenous knowledge skills and bush skills among the Western James Bay Cree women of subarctic Canada. *Human Ecology* **25**: 197-222.

Osherenko, G. 1988. *Sharing Power with Native Users: Co-Management Regimes for Native Wildlife*. Ottawa: Canadian Arctic Resources Committee, Working Paper No. 5.

References

Ostrom, E. 1990. *Governing the Commons: The Evolution of Institutions for Collective Action.* Cambridge: Cambridge University Press.

Ouellet, J.P., D.C. Heard, and S. Boutin. 1993. Range impacts following the introduction of caribou on Southampton Island, Northwest Territories, Canada. *Arctic and Alpine Research* **25(2)**: 136-141.

Overseas Development Administration (ODA). 1996. *Sharing Forest Management: Key Factors, Best Practice, and Ways Forward. Findings from ODA's review of participatory forest management.* London: Overseas Development Administration.

Payne, H. 1998. Personal communication. Executive Director, Manitoba First Nations Elk and Bison Council, Winnipeg, Manitoba.

Payne, H. 1997. *Strategic Business Plan for Manitoba First Nations Elk and Bison Council.* Winnipeg: unpublished report prepared for the Manitoba First Nations Elk and Bison Council by Natural Resources Consulting to First Nations.

Payne, H., H. Nepiak, and K.S.E. Stock. 1993. Waterhen wood bison herd status, in: *Proceedings: North American Public Bison Herds Symposium, 27-29 July 1993, LaCrosse, Wisconsin.*

Picton, H.D. 1991. The history of hunting in North America, pp. 152-156 in Renecker, L.A., and R.J. Hudson (eds.), *Wildlife Production: Conservation and Sustainable Development.* Fairbanks: University of Alaska, AFES misc. publ.: 91-6.

Pimbert, M.P., and J.N. Pretty. 1997. *Diversity and sustainability in community-based conservation.* Paper for the UNESCO-IIPA Regional Workshop on Community-Based Conservation, 9-12 February, India.

Pinkerton, E. (ed.) 1989. *Co-operative Management of Local Fisheries: New Directions for Improved Management and Community Development.* Vancouver: University of British Columbia Press.

Preston, R.J. 1975. *Cree Narrative: Expressing the Personal Meanings of Events.* Ottawa: National Museum of Man Mercury Series, Canadian Ethnology Service, Paper No. 30.

Ramsey, B.J., and A.W. English. 1989. Wild animal harvesting in Australia—an overview, pp. 118-126 in Hudson, R.J., K.R. Drew, and L.M. Baskin (eds.), *Wildlife Production Systems: Economic Utilization of Wild Ungulates.* Cambridge: Cambridge University Press.

Reimer, G., and A. Dialla. 1992. *Community-Based Tourism Development in Pangnirtung, Northwest Territories: Looking Back and Looking Ahead.* Prepared for the GNWT Economic Development and Tourism, Baffin Region, and Hamlet of Pangnirtung.

Renecker, L.A. 1991. Game production: agricultural diversification for Alaska? *Agroborealis* **23(1)**: 20-24.

Renecker, L.A., C.B. Blyth, and C.C. Gates. 1989. Game production in western Canada, pp. 248-267 in Hudson, R.J., K.R. Drew, and L.M. Baskin (eds.), *Wildlife Production Systems: Economic Utilization of Wild Ungulates.* Cambridge: Cambridge University Press.

Riewe, R. 1992. *Nunavut Atlas.* Edmonton: Canadian Circumpolar Institute and Tungavik Federation of Nunavut, Circumpolar Research Series No. 2, 252p.

Roberts, K. 1996. *Circumpolar Aboriginal People and Co-Management Practice: Current Issues in Co-Management and Environmental Assessment.* Calgary: Arctic Institute of North America and Inuvik: Joint Secretariat—Inuvialuit Renewable Resource Committees.

Roberts, K. 1995. *Circumpolar Aboriginal People and Co-Management Practice.* Prepared for the Poster Session on Circumpolar People and Co-Management Practice presented at the Conference of the International Association for the Study of Common Property (IASCP), 24-28 May, Bodø, Norway.

Ross, R. 1992. *Dancing with a Ghost. Exploring Indian Reality.* Markham: Reed Books, Canada.

Royal Commission on Aboriginal Peoples (RCAP). 1996. *Restructuring the Relationship.* Ottawa: Report of the Royal Commission on Aboriginal Peoples, Volume II, Part II.

Scotter, G.W. 1989. Reindeer husbandry in North America, pp. 223-241 in Hudson, R.J., K.R. Drew, and L.M. Baskin (eds.), *Wildlife Production Systems: Economic Utilization of Wild Ungulates.* Cambridge: Cambridge University Press.

Scotter, G.W. 1972. Reindeer ranching in Canada. *Journal of Range Management* **25**: 167-174.

Scotter, G.W., and E.S. Telfer. 1975. *Potential for red meat production from wildlife in boreal and arctic regions.* Ottawa: Circumpolar Conference on Northern Ecology: I23-I24.

Simmons, N., and G. Netro. 1995. Yukon land claims and wildlife management: the cutting edge, pp. 161-174 in Geist, V., and I. McTaggart-Cowan (eds.), *Wildlife Conservation Policy: A Reader.* Calgary: Detselig Enterprises Ltd.

Smith, J.G.E. 1978. Economic uncertainty in an "original affluent society": caribou and caribou-eater Chipewyan adaptive strategies. *Arctic Anthropology* **15**: 68-88.

Smith, M.H. 1995. *Our Home and Native Land? What Governments' Aboriginal Policy is doing to Canada.* Victoria: Crown Western.

Smith, T.G., and D. Taylor. 1977. *Notes on Marine Mammal, Fox, and Polar Bear Harvest in the Northwest Territories, 1940-1972.* Ste. Anne de Bellevue: Department of Fisheries and the Environment, Technical Report No. 694, 37p.

Speck, F.G. 1935. *Naskapi: Savage Hunters of the Labrador Peninsula.* Norman: University of Oklahoma Press.

Speck, F.G. 1915. The family hunting band as the basis of Algonkian social organization. *American Anthropologist* **17**: 289-305.

Stephen, B., R. Glaholt, and L. Little. 1993. *Sachs Harbour-Banks Island Tourism Strategy, 1993-1996.* Yellowknife: Lutra Associated Ltd.

Stern, R.O., E.L. Arobio, L.L. Naylor, and W.C. Thomas. 1980. *Eskimos, Reindeer, and Land.* Fairbanks: University of Alaska, Agriculture Experiment Station Bulletin 59.

Stevenson, M.G. 1997. Ignorance and prejudice threaten environmental assessment. *Policy Options* **March**: 25-28.

References

Stirling, I. 1990. Guest editorial: the future of wildlife management in the Northwest Territories. *Arctic* **43(3)**: iii-iv.

Stock, K.S.E. 1996. *The Traditional Land-Use of Waterhen First Nation vis-à-vis a Forest Management Plan.* Winnipeg: University of Manitoba, M.A. Thesis.

Swerdfager, T.M. 1992. *Cooperative Wildlife Management: A Discussion Paper.* Ottawa: Prepared for the Canadian Wildlife Service.

Tanner, A. 1979. *Bringing Home Animals. Religious Ideology and Mode of Production of the Mistassini Cree Hunter.* London: Hurst.

Thorleifson, I. 1998. Personal communication. Director, Canadian Venison Council, Edmonton, Alberta.

Telfer, E.S., and G.W. Scotter. 1975. Potential for game ranching in boreal aspen forests of western Canada. *Journal of Range Management* **28**: 172-180.

Usher, P.J. 1993. The Beverly-Kaminuriak caribou management board: an experience in co-management, pp. 111-120 in Inglis, J.T. (ed.), *Traditional Ecological Knowledge: Concepts and Cases.* Ottawa: Canadian Museum of Nature, International Program on Traditional Ecological Knowledge and International Development Research Centre.

Usher, P.J. 1991. Some implications of the Sparrow judgement for resource conservation and management. *Alternatives* **18(2)**: 20-21.

Usher, P.J. 1989. *Towards a Strategy for Supporting the Domestic Economy of the Northwest Territories.* Yellowknife: Background study prepared for the NWT Legislative Assembly's Special Committee on the Northern Economy, 66p.

Usher, P.J., 1986. *The Devolution of Wildlife Management and the Prospects for Wildlife Conservation in the Northwest Territories.* Ottawa: Canadian Arctic Resources Committee, Policy Paper No. 3.

Usher, P.J. 1976. Evaluating country food in the northern Native economy. *Arctic* **29**: 105-120.

Usher, P.J., and F.H. Weihs. 1990. *Towards a Strategy for Supporting the Domestic Economy of the Northwest Territories.* Yellowknife: Legislative Assembly of the Northwest Territories. Unpublished report prepared for the Special Committee on the Northern Economy, 64p.

Usher, P.J., and G. Wenzel. 1987. Native harvest surveys and statistics: A critique of their construction and use. *Arctic* **40**: 145-160.

Usher, P.J., D. Delancey, G. Wenzel, M. Smith, and P. White. 1985. *An Evaluation of Native Harvest Survey Methodologies in Northern Canada.* Ottawa: Environmental Studies Revolving Funds Report No. 004, 249p.

Wavey, R. 1993. International workshop on indigenous knowledge and community-based resource management: keynote address, pp. 11-16 in Inglis, J.T. (ed.), *Traditional Ecological Knowledge Systems: Concepts and Cases.* Ottawa: Canadian Museum of Nature, International Program on Traditional Ecological Knowledge and International Development Research Centre.

Wein, E.E., M.M.R. Freeman, and J.C. Markus. 1996. Use of and preference for traditional foods among the Belcher Island Inuit. *Arctic* **49(3)**: 256-264.

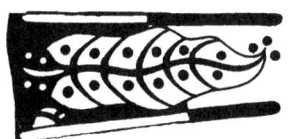 # About the Authors:

Leslie Treseder, Department of Renewable Resources, University of Alberta, Edmonton, Alberta, Canada. Ms. Treseder is a geographer who has worked in wildlife co-management in the context of comprehensive claims. She is completing her M.Sc. degree in Renewable Resources.

Jamie Honda-McNeil, Alberta Environmental Protection, Edmonton, Alberta, Canada. Mr. Honda-McNeil works for the Government of Alberta as a negotiator and policy advisor. He is completing his M.Sc. degree in Renewable Resources at the University of Alberta.

Mina Berkes, c/o Natural Resources Institute, University of Manitoba, Winnipeg, Manitoba, Canada. Dr. M. Berkes is a biologist and consultant living in Winnipeg. She has co-authored two books on environmental and resource conservation and has worked with the Nunavut Wildlife Management Board and Canada's Round Table on the Environment and the Economy.

Fikret Berkes, Natural Resources Institute, University of Manitoba, Winnipeg, Manitoba, Canada. Dr. F. Berkes is Professor of Natural Resources at the University of Manitoba. He has been working in the area of common property resources and community-based management for about 20 years.

Joe Dragon, Department of Renewable Resources, University of Alberta, Edmonton, Alberta, Canada. Mr. Dragon is of Aboriginal descent and was born and raised in Fort Smith, Northwest Territories. He has worked as a wildlife biologist for the GNWT and is currently completing his Ph.D. on the commercial use of wild ungulates in the Northwest Territories, Canada.

Claudia Notzke, Faculty of Management, University of Lethbridge, Lethbridge, Alberta, Canada. Dr. Notzke is a geographer and Associate Professor in the Business Enterprises and Self-Governing Systems (BESS) Program for Indian, Inuit, and Métis Peoples, at the University of Lethbridge. She has conducted research in Canada, the United States, and South Africa and is author of *Aboriginal Peoples and Natural Resources in Canada*.

Tanja Schramm, Department of Renewable Resources, University of Alberta, Edmonton, Alberta, Canada. Ms. Schramm is a geographer and Ph.D. student she has worked with Aboriginal people in northern Australia. She is conducting research on traditional knoweldge of ungulates with First Nations in northern Alberta.

Robert J. Hudson, Faculty of Agriculture, Forestry, and Home Economics, University of Alberta, Edmonton, Alberta, Canada. Dr. Hudson is Associate Dean (Academic Programs) in the Faculty of Agriculture, Forestry, and Home Economics, and Professor of Renewable Resources.

His interests include game ranching and wildlife productivity, as well as community-based wildlife management.

Advisors:

Ms. Dilys Roe, Evaluating Eden Project, International Institute for Environment and Development, London, England.

Dr. Milton M.R. Freeman, H.M. Tory Professor of Anthropology, and Senior Research Scholar, Canadian Circumpolar Institute, University of Alberta, Edmonton, Alberta, Canada.

Dr. Naomi Krogman, Assistant Professor, Department of Rural Economy, University of Alberta, Edmonton, Alberta, Canada.

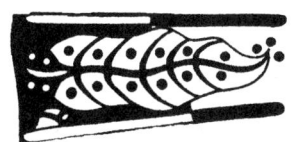

Index

Aboriginal rights, 7-9, 11, 12, 17, 77
Aboriginal title, 9, 12, 13
access rights, 2
adventure tourism, 55
animal rights movement, 59
antler velvet, 71, 75, 76
arts and craft, 58, 62
assimilation policy, 10, 11, 20, 77
Berger Commission, 29, 33
Beverly-Qamanirjuaq Caribou
    Management Board (BQCMB), 15
big game hunting (see hunting)
bird life, 35
Boundary Extension Act, 14
breeding stock, 71, 73, 76
British North America Act, 9, 10
Calder case, 12
Canadian Confederation, 9
Canadian Constitution Act, 17, 77
carrying capacity, 39, 67
Charter of Indian Rights, 9
co-management (see also wildlife)
    community-based, 11, 16, 18, 21
    -25, 33, 57
    boards, 14, 15, 20, 38
commercial harvesting, 35, 43, 69
common-property, 32, 46
communal territory, 26
community economic development, 34, 39, 41, 43, 51, 71, 77-80
community hunts, 37-39
Comprehensive Claim(s), 2, 3, 9, 11, 13, 15, 16, 20, 22, 31, 32, 36, 38, 47, 51, 52, 56, 69, 77
    Champagne and Aishihik Agreement, 19
    Gwich'in Agreement, 19
    Inuvialuit Final Agreement, 14, 19, 53, 69
    James Bay and Northern Quebec Agreement, 13-14, 19, 36
    Nacho Nyak Dun Agreement, 19
    Northeastern Quebec Agreement, 19
    Nunavut Agreement, 14, 19, 27
    Sahtu Dene and Métis Agreement, 19
    Teslin Tlingit Agreement, 19
    Vuntut Gwichin, 19
conservation, 2, 14, 17, 25, 45, 53, 57, 62, 80
Crown land, 11, 14, 32
cultural identity, 27-29, 33, 41, 43, 75
cultural tours, 56
dog team, 52, 54
    rides, 61
domestic livestock, 73
economic diversification, 65
economy
    cash, 31
    commercial/export, 35, 42
    domestic, 29, 35, 49, 78
    land-based, 25, 29, 34, 37, 55, 59, 60, 62-63
    local/regional, 58
    mixed, 9, 24, 29, 34-35, 48-49, 59-60, 78-79
    non-traditional, 31
    subsistence, 24, 31, 80
    traditional, 24, 31, 32
    wage, 25, 29, 34, 42
ecotourism, 34, 47, 55, 57, 58, 60, 63, 64, 76, 80
empowerment, 20, 33, 46, 58
endangered species, 1, 73, 74
environmental impacts, 21, 56
exotic foods, 43
fish, 30, 35, 46, 61
fishing, 51, 61
    rights, 17
food safety, 42, 43, 45
forestry, 33
free-roaming ungulates, 35, 39, 41, 44, 65, 67, 69, 70, 73
fur trade, 23, 25, 26, 41
game farming, 65, 67, 72, 73, 75
game ranching, 3, 65, 70, 71, 75, 79, 80
geese, 24, 30, 61
grazing grounds, 69
guided hunts, 71, 75
habitat management, 1
harvesting, 24
herding, 36, 67, 69
homestay programs, 59, 63
Hudson's Bay Company, 10, 23

hunt ranches, 75
hunter/gatherer society, 9, 35
Hunters' and Trappers'
  Associations, Committees, and/or Organizations 38, 39, 52, 53
hunting
  big game, 30, 52, 53, 55, 61, 80
  commercial, 3, 35-42, 44, 46, 79, 80
  pressure, 26
  rights, 2, 3, 7, 14, 17, 26, 32, 36, 52, 76, 77, 79
  sports hunting, 51-56, 61-62, 76, 80
  territories, 24, 25
hydro-electric projects, 33
Indian, 2, 7, 18, 30, 33, 35
  non-status, 2
Indian Act of 1876, 10, 12
intellectual property rights, 21
Inuit, 2, 7, 18, 27, 30, 35
Inuvialuit Settlement Region, 38
James Bay hydro-electric project, 14
kinship, 28
land tenure systems, 25
land use, 24, 25, 27, 32, 34, 77, 79
leakage, 61, 62
livestock diversification, 66, 72, 75
marine mammals, 30, 35
  whales, 35, 46, 59-61
  seals, 35
  Marine Mammal Protection Act, 52
market hunting, 37, 38
market opportunities, 34
Métis, 2, 18
mining, 33
multiple stakeholders, 15, 20, 46, 62
non-renewable resources, 10
northern development, 13, 21, 23, 29, 34, 42
oriental antler market, 69
oriental medicine, 71
outdoor adventure, 52
outfitting, 34, 52, 53, 55, 58
partnerships, 20, 46, 62
private enterprise, 1
protected areas, 51, 56, 57, 79
ptarmigan, 30
pulse hunts, 40
quotas, 37, 38, 40, 45, 46, 53
regulatory agencies, 21
religious activity, 27
reservation, 9, 10, 68
River rafting, 61
Royal Proclamation of 1763, 8, 9, 13
sealing industry, 42

seedstock, 73
self-government , 16, 20, 33
socio-economic impacts, 21, 58
Sparrow Case, 17
Specific claims, 13
squatting, 9
subsistence, 15, 23, 24, 31, 32, 37, 41, 61, 68
  activities, 1, 32, 34, 42, 78, 79
  economy, 24, 29, 31, 79
  hunting, 3, 23, 24, 27-30, 33, 37, 45-46, 51, 60-61, 77-80
survey techniques, 16
sustainability, 44, 45, 57, 64, 76
total allowable harvest, 38, 45
tourism
  activities, 51, 55, 58-61, 79
  Community-Based Tourism Strategy, 47
traditional
  culture, 10, 32-33, 39-41, 65, 70, 75
  diet, 70
  economy, 24, 29, 31-34
  hunting, 36, 38, 51, 52
  territories, 12
  use, 13
traditional ecological knowledge (TEK), 15, 20-22, 27, 28, 75
transfer payments, 1, 25, 31, 49, 78
Treaties, 2, 8, 12, 13, 33
  Nisga'a, 12, 19
  Two Row Wampum, 8
wage employment, 1, 25, 31, 42, 48, 78
waterfowl, 30
White Paper on Indian Policy, 11
wildlife
  management/co-management, 1-3, 7,7,13-16, 21, 70,77
  resources, 1, 2, 7
  species
    beaver, 26, 30
    bison, 15, 66-68, 73, 75
    caribou, 15, 28, 30, 36-39, 42, 44-45, 52, 55, 61, 68
    deer, 66
    grizzly bear, 52, 53, 61
    moose, 15, 30, 66
    muskoxen, 35, 39-45, 52-54, 61, 67
    polar bears, 35, 52-54, 61, 62
    reindeer, 35, 66-68
    snowshoe hare, 30
    wapiti (elk), 66, 71, 72, 75
  tourism, 3, 47-50, 61, 64, 80
  viewing, 50, 51, 56, 80

92